Haunted Healthcare

Also by Richard Estep

In Search of the Paranormal
Haunted Longmont
The World's Most Haunted Hospitals
Trail of Terror
Colorado UFOs
The Devil's Coming to Get Me
The Fairfield Haunting

As co-author

The Haunting of Asylum 49
Spirits of the Cage

Haunted Healthcare

Medical Professionals and Patients Share
Their Encounters with the Paranormal

Richard Estep

Copyright 2018 Richard Estep

All rights reserved

For Kyle,

One of the kindest, gentlest, and most courageous young men it has ever been my honor to meet.

You, sir, are my hero.

Contents

Foreword by Chris Balassone
Introduction
Chapter 1 – The Girl with the Glowing Red Eyes
Chapter 2 – Death in the Basement
Chapter 3 – Major Trauma
Chapter 4 – Help Me Breathe
Chapter 5 – The Tunnels
Chapter 6 – A Last Goodbye
Chapter 7 – Graveyard Nightmares
Chapter 8 – The Seventh Floor
Chapter 9 – It's Only Natural to be Afraid
Chapter 10 – A Sixth Sense?
Chapter 11 – The Departing Soul
Chapter 12 – Fatal Mistakes
Chapter 13 – The Man in the Body Bag
Chapter 14 – The Lady in White
Chapter 15 – Escaping our Demons
Chapter 16 – A Call for Help
Chapter 17 – A Prankster in the Morgue
Chapter 18 – The Bravest Yeti
Acknowledgments

Foreword

Most people think healthcare workers are there to save lives and help people. What they don't think about is the death that they see day in and day out. Along with that come experiences that they cannot explain and rarely want to talk about — or at least, that's the way it used to be.

Now that the paranormal is becoming more widely accepted, the more stories are coming to light, and the more comfortable healthcare workers are becoming in sharing those stories.

I first started out in the medical field some twenty-five years ago as an EMT, then moved on to become a nurse, and have now been a paramedic for the past fourteen years. During that time, I have seen many things that I cannot explain. Having been a paranormal investigator for more than ten years, I will pay greater attention to these situations than most people, and therefore I tend to acknowledge them more quickly.

Sharing these stories can actually be helpful in two different ways. The first is that reading and acknowledging them can help those people who take care of us feel better about their own paranormal experiences. The second is that these accounts give us more information as investigators to help get some answers that we haven't yet gotten concerning the nature of the paranormal and the afterlife.

The stories that you are about to read don't just come from healthcare professionals; they come from patients as well. There will of course be skeptics who simply dismiss it all out of hand, saying something along the lines of: "Meh, those patients were on medications, and they were probably experiencing hallucinations and other side-effects." That is indeed a possibility, but this is the patient's own personal experience, and that is all that matters at the end of the day.

One commonly accepted theory holds that spirits, ghosts, and most other types of paranormal activity need energy in order to manifest. Well, just take a look at all of the energy that can be found in a hospital, or any other kind of healthcare facility. Energy doesn't simply dissipate; it only changes form, and that would make any hospital a potential hotbed for paranormal activity.

Think about all of the traumatic events, the strong emotions (both good and bad) and not to mention the wide range of electrical medical equipment…all of these things happen on a daily basis, and can just be absorbed into the walls and environment of the location, just waiting for the right conditions to arise — and then it all comes back out.

When it comes to the experiences of first responders, I take those even more to heart – most likely because I happen to be one myself. We are the men and women who see the most horrific events, being with people in their very last minute of life, when we are doing everything humanly possible to try and save them. It is an extremely stressful, high energy situation, and can be extremely traumatic for everybody involved.

Think about all of the raw emotional energy that exists in the back of the ambulance while all this is going on. What's to say that this energy doesn't remain in the rig afterward, either staying anchored in place there or, perhaps every bit as likely, it could come out once the ambulance gets back to the firehouse or its home base…and now people are wondering why it is that the building has suddenly developed paranormal activity. Just a thought…

The stories that you will read in this book are actual occurrences that the healthcare providers and patients have experienced firsthand. How do you think you would react if you found yourself in one of these situations? Although they aren't necessarily talked about openly, these things happen on a very regular basis in the healthcare profession. It doesn't matter whether it takes place in the hospital, in a nursing home, or even out on the street — when something paranormal occurs, it can startle even the most experienced provider, often making them question just what it was they believe that they saw or experienced.

There are some long-abandoned places that are no longer open as a functioning medical facility, but *are* open for paranormal investigations…places such as Asylum 49 in Utah, or Waverly Hills Sanatorium in Kentucky. Just because many of the paranormal experiences happened while the facility was open, does not necessarily mean that they stopped when the doors closed for the last time. As a paranormal investigator, that is very good news, because we can listen to the accounts told by eyewitnesses and possibly even experience the same thing that the person did who is sharing their story with us. If nothing else it gives us a good starting point for our investigation.

I have personally had a couple of experiences while on duty as well (of course, I have had most of my experiences as a paranormal investigator while off-duty).

One of the more bizarre experiences happened when I was a 16-year-old EMT working at a volunteer rescue squad. It was a rainy night, and we had just gone out to eat dinner when we got the call. It was for a car into a tree, with injuries (the tree always seems to win).

Even all these years later, I can distinctly remember munching on my taco on the way to the call, thinking that I should eat it now or I may not be able to eat it at all. When we got there, the fire department was already on-scene, and as I pulled up in my vehicle, I could see that a 14 year-old boy was lying on the ground with the fire guys working on him.

I jumped out and immediately began helping. Right away, I knew this was going to be a bad one: he was in a traumatically-induced cardiac arrest. Statistically, less than two percent of those patients survive. We scooped him up and ran hot to the hospital with lights and sirens going. All the while, I was doing CPR.

The emergency department doctors pronounced him dead not long after we arrived. That was my first field death, and he was only two years younger than me. After giving it a lot of thought, I decided that I would go to his viewing.

Two days before the viewing, the dead boy came to me in my dreams and told me not to worry. He said that he knew we did everything we possibly could for him, and most importantly, that he was okay now.

I went the viewing a couple of days later, and as I walked up to his coffin, he smiled and said "thank you." Every hair on my body stood on end. I may have looked calm on the outside, but on the inside, I was absolutely panic-stricken. Quickly turning around, I walked right on out of the funeral home without ever looking back.

I will never forget either the call or the experience.

Richard Estep is an established author, experienced paranormal investigator, veteran paramedic, and a good friend. In the following stories he will make you feel like you are actually there, living and experiencing it for yourself. Every word will have you wanting more and keep you on the edge of your seat from cover to cover. This book is one of the latest books in a series he has written that covers not just the intersection of healthcare and hauntings, but also the haunting of places that range from the very well-known to the private and obscure.

With those books, he is writing about his own personal experiences, as he likes to actually move into the location in order to find out for himself, often for days at a time. There isn't anyone better who could not only accurately tell the stories of these people, but also to do it in such a way as to make them accessible, easy to understand, and feel completely real to the reader.

Richard puts everything into his writing, and it shows the passion he has for bringing these stories to life. If this is your first book of Richard's, I can guarantee that it won't be your last.

Enjoy your trip into the ghostly realm of Haunted Healthcare!

Chris Balassone
The Paranormal Paramedic

Introduction

All places and professions have their ghosts.

Over the course of my 24-year career as a paranormal investigator, I have encountered many reports of ghosts and hauntings that occurred in such places as hotels, offices, shops and stores of every variety. These experiences have happened to people of all ages and those who come from all walks of life.

Yet when taken as a whole, it is fair to say that the great majority of truly compelling cases seem to have centered upon the medical profession, and those who are associated with it, whether they happen to be patients or care providers. There seems to be an indefinable something about those places of healing and the people within them that has some kind of affinity for the paranormal.

During the research and writing of my third book, *The World's Most Haunted Hospitals*, I spoke with a plethora of doctors, nurses, patients, and paranormal investigators about their ghostly experiences. Personally, I find healthcare providers to be some of the most compelling and convincing eyewitnesses to paranormal phenomena; they come from an educational background that is steeped in the physical sciences, and are taught from the very first stages of their careers how to think critically. It was surprising (and more than a little funny) to see just how many supposedly-skeptical doctors and nurses told me something along the lines of: "I don't believe in the paranormal, ghosts, or anything like that...but *this one time*..." They would then go on to tell me a hair-raising story involving some ghostly encounter, usually one for which they had no rational explanation, and something that they simply shrugged off nonchalantly before getting on with their lives.

One of my first brushes with the paranormal occurred in 2002, when I was serving as a volunteer firefighter-EMT in my adopted state of Colorado. It had been a quiet night, with only a few 911 calls for our fire engine to run. I was kicking back and watching a little late-night TV upstairs in the crew quarters with one of my fellow firefighters when we suddenly heard the sound of footsteps coming from beneath us. Puzzled, we looked at one another with raised eyebrows. Who would be walking around in the vehicle bay at this time of night? It was close to midnight, and the rest of the engine company were all tucked up in their bunk beds, waiting for the next alarm to drop.

This wasn't too long after the horrific events of 9/11, and

we as a department were all very security conscious, so we both got out of our recliners and went downstairs to check. Perhaps one of the volunteers had come by to drop off some equipment, I thought.

Just as we reached the bottom of the stairs, we heard the sound of a door slamming — not one of the heavy doors of the building entrances, but rather the more metallic noise of a fire apparatus door being slammed shut with a *ker-clunk*.

The engine bay was completely dark. Reaching out, I flipped on the lights. Not a thing was moving in there. The bright red fire engines, wildland brush trucks and water tenders were all parked nose-to-tail, ready to go out whenever the tones went off. Our jackets, boots and bunker pants sat next to the primary response engine, in readiness for us to jump into when the call came.

Of living people, however, there was no sign at all. Just to be sure, we walked along the rows of vehicles, looking inside each cab and even underneath the chassis to make sure that nobody was hiding in the shadows — not that it was likely, but we figured it was better to be safe than sorry. Over the course of the next quarter-hour, we searched high and low, ensuring that no intruder was lurking in the bay.

We came up totally empty. With a shrug that felt ever so slightly uneasy, we both went back to watching the movie.

I have always had a tendency to snore like a chain-saw, so as a courtesy to my fellow firefighters, I usually slept on the couch in the TV room rather than inflict that special brand of misery upon them. After the movie had finished, I stretched out on the couch and killed the lights.

Normally, we would have been woken up during the night whenever the alarms went off, but this just happened to be an unusually slow night. I slept like the dead, no pun intended.

Until…

Somebody was tapping me on top of the head. It was the sort of insistent *tap-tap-tap* that seemed to say, "Hey, wake up, you idiot!"

My eyes flew open.

"Oh, shit!" I said, thinking that I had overslept and missed shift changeover. It was a big no-no to sleep through your alarm and miss the crew change, which was one of the most important parts of the firehouse day; it was the time and place for us to exchange information with the oncoming firefighters, let them know whatever we thought they needed to know, and then shoot the breeze a little. Firefighters had been known to wake up sleepy-heads in some pretty inventive ways, all of which were loud, unpleasant, and usually very embarrassing. Many of them involved freezing cold water.

With a jolt, I was suddenly wide awake. Sitting up, I looked around me, fully expecting to find one of my fellow firefighters standing there, angry at having to get my lazy ass out of bed. Shift changeover happened at seven o'clock in the morning, so it should have been daylight outside, but behind the window blinds I could see only darkness. The TV room was empty, apart from myself, and the only thing I could hear was the sound of my own heart beating loudly in my ears.

I asked myself whether I could have dreamed the whole thing, but quickly discounted the possibility. The tapping on my head had been very real, and firm enough to pull me out of a dead sleep instantly. This was no hypnopompic hallucination, a symptom of my own brain tricking me just as I was in the process of waking up. I'd gone from a dead sleep to wide awake in the space of a second or two, and could still practically feel those fingers tapping me on top of my head.

Looking at my watch, I noted that the time was a little

after five o'clock. Figuring that there was no sense in going back to sleep now, I got up, packed my bedding away, and went downstairs to the table. The experience had been vaguely disconcerting, and I made a point of reporting it to the captain on duty, who looked at me in a funny way but said nothing more about it. The fire station didn't have a reputation for being haunted, although a few months before, one of the firefighters had claimed that a child's toy had moved across the bunk room on its own. Pretty much everybody had written that off as being a tall story or practical joke. There were no ghost stories associated with the building that I was aware of.

Shift changeover came and went. I took a little good-natured ribbing from the boys, which I had been expecting. It was pretty much par for the course at any firehouse when something out of the ordinary happened.

Driving home, my feeling of unease never quite went away. When I walked through the front door, I found that my wife at the time was in tears.

"What's wrong?" I asked, setting down my bag and giving her a big hug.

"It's my mom," she said. "I just got the phone call. She died this morning, at about five o'clock…"

As ghost stories go, this experience is far from atypical. The annals of paranormal research are filled with instances in which, at the moment of their death, a dying person is seen, heard, or otherwise experienced (sometimes in dreams) by their loved ones. I was very fond of my mother-in-law, and her passing deeply saddened me. It's fair to say that we had a strong emotional connection, and that particular type of bond seems to be a prerequisite for a death-bed encounter such as this.

Did her spirit actually pay me a visit at the fire house in order to say goodbye one last time, or did some part of me that I cannot name somehow sense her passing? It is impossible to say. Skeptics would also point out that the timing of my experience, coinciding as it did with the time of my mother-in-law's death almost exactly, could easily be put down to nothing more than simple coincidence — to which I would say that after having investigated claims of the paranormal for so many years on both sides of the Atlantic, my willingness to ascribe such things to coincidence has been greatly diminished. Time and time again, we see such bizarre experiences dismissed as being 'purely coincidental,' but there must come a point at which one has to rely too heavily on that tired old explanation for it to ring true.

Although I cannot prove it beyond all shadow of a doubt, it is my firm belief that she was dropping in to say one last good-bye…and I feel very fortunate to have gotten that opportunity. After all, not everybody is that lucky. `

I had only been working in the field of emergency medicine for a short period of time when I had that particular experience, but I was already a seasoned paranormal investigator. As the years went by, I ran into more than my fair share of EMTs, paramedics, nurses, physician and nursing assistants, doctors, and countless others involved in the healthcare field — a great many of whom were actual patients, rather than professionals — that had encountered something they believed to be ghostly in nature. The possibility of writing those experiences down and putting them into print was always lurking in the back of mind, but it would not come to fruition until I met an extraordinary young man named Kyle.

You will read Kyle's fascinating and inspiring story in its entirety later on in this book, so I will not go into the details now — suffice it to say that he is one of the bravest human beings it has ever been my fortune to meet, as are his parents and sister, Megan. As I sat at Kyle's bedside and listened to him describe his experiences in a very matter-of-fact way, I knew that I had to share them with a wider audience; not only because they are utterly compelling, but because courage such as Kyle's should not go unrecognized.

So, sit back, dear reader, and make yourself comfortable. Our journey into the realm of haunted medicine is about to begin.

Richard Estep
Longmont, Colorado
September 2018

CHAPTER ONE
The Girl with the Glowing Red Eyes

Robbin is a highly experienced nurse of many years' standing. She has worked in many different aspects of nursing care over the course of her career, including what is arguably the most challenging and heart-breaking field of them all, that of pediatric palliative nursing – taking care of dying children.

It takes a very special sort of person to do that kind of work. As a paramedic, I have taken a number of children on what we call 'hospice transports' over the years. The knowledge that the little one lying in front of you on the ambulance gurney is dying, and will almost certainly never get to grow up or enjoy another Christmas, is nothing short of gut-wrenching. For the EMT or paramedic, those calls only last for an hour or two at most, and then we are on to the next emergency…although they do tend to keep you awake in the wee small hours of the morning. They are mercifully infrequent, and yet when they *do* come along, the dying children are the ones that stay with you forever.

How much harder must it be for the nurses and other end-of-life medical professionals, who spend most of their working week tending to such patients? Although I am not a religious man, I truly believe that people such as this are the closest thing we have to angels, walking the earth in human form. I just can't comprehend how those compassionate men and women can deal with such heartbreak every day, day in and day out, and still remain centered and even upbeat. My hat goes off to all of the end-of-life carers that I have encountered during the course of my medical career. To me, every one of them is a hero.

In addition to being one of the finest nurses I know, Robbin is also a very good friend of mine, and I trust her word and her judgment absolutely. As a gifted psychic medium and paranormal investigator, Robbin has over ten years investigating haunted locations with me, along with her husband, Randy. She has produced some remarkable 'hits' while on investigations, and can always be relied upon to keep a level head when things turn dark and scary.

Robbin and I were sitting in a haunted jail cell late one evening, just waiting around for something to happen, and I asked her what cases she was working on at the moment. She told me that she was currently a little preoccupied with something that was happening at her place of employment, a nursing facility for the elderly and those who could not take care of themselves.

Her story, when she told it, was nothing short of terrifying.

At the time these events occurred, Robbin was working as a weekend nursing manager. One of her duties was to organize the schedule, making sure that the nursing home was staffed appropriately — and if that wasn't possible, she had to work the unfilled shifts herself. Unsurprisingly, the toughest shifts to fill were the overnights on weekends; not many people want to voluntarily work on Friday, Saturday, or Sunday nights.

The facility housed somewhere around sixty residents, all of whom were taken care of by nurses and nurse aides. Robbin arrived one night to work an overnight shift that she just hadn't been able to fill. She took a hand-off report from the off-going evening shift nurse, who told her that one of the patients, who lived in a room at the end of a long hallway, had been hallucinating rather badly that evening. This news didn't faze Robbin particularly. The lady was in her eighties, and suffered with dementia. Hallucinations are not uncommon in such instances.

What *was* unusual was that the old lady had begun to growl at the nursing staff when they went in to attend to her needs.

"Have you tried giving her a change of scene?" Robbin asked. "Getting her out of that room and into a recliner in the common room might help her a little bit."

"The aide wouldn't help me," the other nurse admitted, sounding a little embarrassed. "She said 'whatever's in there, I don't want it coming home with me…'"

Robbin blinked in surprise. *Whatever's in there?* What a strange expression for a nursing professional to use.

"What exactly did she mean by that?"

The nurse proceeded to tell Robbin that she and the nursing aide believed the old woman to be possessed. For her part, Robbin was unconvinced, reasoning that the growling was most likely a worsening of her dementia symptoms.

With the hand-off taken care off, the evening shift staff left, leaving Robbin in charge of the building. After making her rounds to check in on the patients, most of whom appeared to be sleeping soundly, she went back to the nurse's station and set about climbing the small mountain of administrative paperwork she still had left to complete.

It was close to two o'clock in the morning when she looked up from her desk. The sound of a loud, throaty growl echoed along one of the hallways. A deep and threatening rumble, she could tell that it had come from inside the troubled old lady's room, audible even through the closed door.

Instantly, Robbin became convinced that this was something more than dementia. There was an inhuman quality to the growl that made the hairs on the back of her neck stand on end.

Nevertheless, she was a nurse and she had a patient to care for. It was that simple. Getting up from her chair, she made her way down the hallway toward the door at the far end.

With every step she took, the growling seemed to get louder and more intense.

Reaching out a hand, she twisted the handle and pushed the door open slowly. The room was completely dark. As she stepped inside, Robbin was hit with an overwhelming sense of oppression and heaviness. Each step she took felt as if she was swimming underwater.

"The atmosphere in this room was nothing short of *horrible*," she recalled afterward from the comfort of our jail cell. "I've been a paranormal investigator for nearly a quarter of a century. It takes a *lot* to scare me, but I did *not* want to be in that room. It took everything I had not to turn around and leave that room immediately."

As a paranormal investigator, she would certainly have been able to do that. Few would have faulted her for it. As a nurse, however, she did not. There was a patient in her charge, and that meant she had a duty to care for her. Fleeing was not an option.

The old lady was lying in bed, her head and shoulders propped up against a pile of pillows. She let out yet another loud growl, one that set Robbin's teeth on edge like nails on a chalkboard. Using her most soothing tone of voice, Robbin asked her gently what was wrong.

"It's the girl."

"What girl?" Robbin frowned.

The old lady lifted a hand and pointed toward the floor.

"The little girl with the red eyes. She's hiding under my bed…"

Squatting down on her haunches, Robbin looked underneath the bed. Finding it to be empty, she reassured her patient that there was nobody under there. But the woman was insistent. The girl had glowing red eyes, she repeated, and had crawled under the bed to hide when Robbin had entered the room. She gave a very detailed physical description of the girl, all the way down to the dress she was wearing.

Robbin went to fetch the nurse aide, telling her that she needed a little help. Just as the evening shift aide had refused to go into that room, the same was true of her night shift counterpart.

"What's got you so spooked?" Robbin asked. "Is it the growling?"

"She keeps talking about a little girl with red eyes hiding in the room, underneath her bed," the aide explained. That stopped Robbin dead in her tracks. She knew from experience that the resident in question had very severe memory issues. It wasn't at all unusual for a nurse to go into her room, introduce herself by name, spend a minute or two administering some medications, and then have the old lady ask what her name was again. She would forget things that had happened just moments ago.

Yet if the aide's story was correct, the resident had been telling the same story for the past few hours. Robbin asked the aide to repeat the old lady's description of the red-eyed girl. It matched *exactly* with what she had just told Robbin. This was unusually good recall for a patient who could barely remember anything for more than two or three minutes at a time.

But the aide wasn't done yet. She said that the elderly resident was also seeing a headless woman in her room, standing in the corner and not moving.

Robbin went back to the resident's room with the very reluctant aide in tow. Just as the aide had said, she was now pointing into one of the dark corners, babbling about the lady with no head. Robbin and the aide could see nobody back there, but both of them were afflicted by an extremely oppressive sensation from the moment they crossed the threshold.

They tucked the old lady up under her blankets and sat with her until she finally fell asleep.

Robbin somehow ended up working several more days in a row. Over the course of the following week, she found that the memory-impaired resident kept telling her the exact same story. The red-eyed little girl under the bed and the headless woman in the corner of the room popped up again and again, and the details were always the same — perfectly consistent with what she had been saying all along.

"The little girl was nice at first," the old lady told

Robbin tearfully during one of her more lucid intervals. "But now she's gotten mean. She's telling me to do things. *Bad things…*"

"What is she telling you to do?" Robbin asked gently, taking her hand.

"She wants me to hit you. To hurt you."

This didn't faze Robbin too much. It is sadly quite common for patients such as this to lash out at their loved ones and caregivers. They aren't by any means bad or violent people by nature, most of the time; it is simply one of the side-effects of their illness, one which often gets worse as their mental faculties decline.

The medical staff at the facility did their best to treat this with medication, including the use of an antipsychotic named haloperidol (its name is usually shortened to Haldol). Unfortunately, the medication didn't have much of an effect on the growling lady, whose angry episodes only seemed to grow worse. One of the nursing staff pointed out that the resident, who was usually a very sweet and friendly woman, hadn't begun to growl and see phantom figures until after she had been moved into that specific room.

After their trial of medication had failed, the patient's doctors tried every diagnostic test in the book in their attempts to try and diagnose the cause of her increasingly frequent hallucinations, including CT scans of her brain. Nothing obvious jumped out at them. Was her dementia simply worsening…or could there perhaps have been another course?

One day, Robbin was helping the troubled old lady take her medications. Suddenly, the patient's head snapped around to look at one corner of the room. Her tone became one of panic. When Robbin asked her what was wrong, the now-terrified woman told her that *they* were back.

"They?" Robbin asked. "Who are 'they'?"

"The *things!*"

When pressed gently for more details, she went on to describe nightmarish creatures that were a cross between a spider and a human being. These spider-things had been coming into her room for days now, she claimed, crawling up and down the walls. There were always three of them, no more, no less, and they quite understandably frightened the life out of her. Every once in a while, one of the creatures would scuttle across the floor to sit next to her bed, where it would claw at her with one of its appendages.

As if this wasn't terrifying enough, the creatures then began to growl back at her, and in her words, "told me to do such very bad things…"

The old lady could not even remember the name of her own daughter, yet as the days passed, she continued to tell Robbin and the other nurses this exact same story over and over again, always with perfect consistency. Small wonder that they began to get scared when they were around her, eyeing the walls of the room warily.

A short while later, Robbin noticed that the nature of her patient's growls was starting to change. It was almost as if there were two different voices growling in tandem, competing for supremacy. Neither one sounded as if it could possibly have emanated from such a frail and delicate voice box — there was a definite masculine quality to each one.

Thankfully, she was living in a single bedroom, so there was no possibility of putting a room-mate in there with her. One can only imagine how stressful and downright frightening it would have been to have shared a room with her!

No matter how hard she tried, Robbin was unable to calm her patient down in the slightest, let alone get her to stop growling. The nurse aide flatly refused to go into the room any more, something for which Robbin could hardly blame her. It felt as if, rather than a sweet little old lady, they were being confronted by an animal…or something worse.

Finally, at a complete loss for what to do, she stepped outside and phoned her husband, Randy, a fellow paranormal investigator.

"I don't know where he is, but can you please track down Stephen and ask him to pray for us?"

Stephen was also a paranormal investigator, one who just so happened to be a priest who specialized in handling those cases that were darker and more malevolent than the standard everyday type of haunting. If anybody could help out, even from a distance, it would be him.

With her request made, Robbin went back inside and stood just outside the patient's doorway. Closing her eyes, she began to pray quietly, focusing on the fervent hope that her patient be granted some measure of respite from whatever force it was — whether medical, paranormal, or some degree of both — that afflicted her.

Unbeknownst to Robbin, her husband had managed to reach Stephen in a very timely manner. The priest immediately began to offer up prayers for Robbin and her patient from his home in the mountains, while she did the very same thing from right outside the patient's door.

Their combined efforts appear to have worked, and

worked quickly. Almost as if a switch had been flipped, the old woman stopped growling and flopped backward onto her pillows. As she looked at Robbin, her expression changed from a malicious scowl to one of warmth and friendliness.

"Hi honey," she said with a smile, "can I please have some hot chocolate?"

Robbin blinked, taken aback. It appeared as though she was looking at a completely different person than she had been just a few seconds ago. Every last ounce of aggression had suddenly melted away, leaving the kindly old lady once more in its place.

At the time of writing, she is doing a little better. The episodes of growling are fewer and farther between, as are the visits from the spider-people she claims to have.

But even though things are calming down somewhat as far as this particular patient is concerned, there are other reports of paranormal activity at the same nursing home.

Staff have heard themselves called out to at night when working alone in the offices, when nobody else is around or awake. The lights appear to have taken on a life of their own, flickering far beyond what would seem reasonable for even the oldest of wiring, and even switching themselves off and on when the mood takes them. Most of these lights are controlled by motion sensors, which means that something tangible must be triggering them in order to turn the lights on — even when there is nobody up and about.

Robbin has learned to deal with these shenanigans by telling the culprit to knock it off, which usually happens. When she leaves the office building in order to tend to her duties and then returns later on, the doors leading to the conference room like to open themselves up of their own accord. This somehow manages to take place without any of the motion sensor-activated lights being triggered, which should be impossible if a living, breathing, flesh and blood person was responsible.

Finally, she decided to mention it to her boss, who said, "Yeah, we've noticed that too. We just don't like to talk about it…"

Speaking as an avowed agnostic, I find prayer to be a very interesting thing indeed. Some people, usually those of an atheistic persuasion, like to dismiss it as being nothing more than mere wishful thinking.

They point to cases in which a great many people were praying for a disaster to be averted or for a person to survive, only to have their prayers go unanswered. While a theological discussion is beyond the scope of this book, I would like to point out that prayer may have a similar effect to a well-documented phenomenon from the medical field: the placebo effect.

The medical community still isn't entirely sure how the placebo effect works, only that it *does* work in many cases. Indeed, it is an extremely powerful therapy when applied correctly and under the proper circumstances.

A lot of misconceptions exist about what the placebo effect is capable of. It certainly isn't a universal panacea or cure-all. It is not capable of reversing the spread of cancerous cells or mitigating the tissue damage caused by a heart attack, for example. Where placebo really shines is those aspects of physical being that are modulated by the brain, such as pain control or the feeling of nausea. Doctors believe that the effect fosters a closer relationship between the mind and the body, which results in a beneficial outcome for both.

Could prayer do the same thing – in other words, is it a form of 'spiritual placebo?' It's unlikely, in my opinion, though still possible. Robbin's patient may have been aware that her nurse was praying for her, but could not possibly have known that Stephen was also, as he was situated many miles away at the time. There is also the fact that Robbin was standing outside the patient's closed door, and the patient most likely could not have heard her in the first place.

This leaves us with two possibilities, broadly speaking. Either the patient's sudden turnaround was a pure coincidence, or the prayers offered up by Stephen and Robbin did indeed work, but in a way in which we cannot explain.

Skeptics will most likely accept the former explanation, and believers will probably go with the latter. As for me, well…I believe that the jury is still out.

CHAPTER TWO
Death in the Basement

Many years ago, Robbin was working as a home hospice nurse. This involved taking care of the dying in their own place of residence, with the goal of allowing them to pass away as peacefully and comfortably as possible at home. If given the choice, who wouldn't prefer to end their days in familiar surroundings with their pets and loved ones all around them?

She saw more than her fair share of strange things during this particular part of her career, and not all of them were paranormal in nature.

For example, it was often necessary for the home hospice nurses to pronounce a patient dead. This involved confirming that there were no signs of life, such as a pulse, spontaneous breathing, or central nervous system activity – for example, any movement of the pupils or a purposeful response to reflex testing.

Once they were satisfied that the patient was indeed deceased, the nurse would document an official time of death, which was the time that would ultimately be entered upon their death certificate. Then they would call the appropriate funeral home and ask them to come and pick up the body.

One night, Robbin was called out to attend upon a Chinese family whose grandfather had died peacefully in his sleep. After knocking on the door and exchanging solemn but polite pleasantries with one of his children, she was shown into the master bedroom. There she found a small, frail-looking old man, lying on his back in the middle of a huge water bed.

Knowing that she needed to check for a pulse and listen for a heartbeat, Robbin looped her stethoscope about her neck and climbed carefully up onto the bed. She shuffled forward on hands and knees toward the center of the bed. A series of rippling waves preceded her across the mattress. It was all she could do not to get sea-sick. The rolling motion was making her queasy.

Just as she reached her patient and placed a hand on his wrist, the old gentleman's eyes fluttered open. So did his mouth. He said, *"Oh!"*

It took every last ounce of self-control Robbin had not to scream and leap off the bed in shock. For his part, the patient *did* scream. Who could blame him, opening his eyes to find a stranger crawling across the bed toward him with a look of intense determination on her face?

As things turned out, her patient hadn't been dead at all — his family had mistaken a very deep sleep state for that of the ultimate, final type of repose, and had called for a hospice nurse prematurely.

The patient may not have been dead, but he came perilously close to giving Robbin a heart attack of her own. Looking back on it now, with the benefit of hindsight, she is able to laugh at what happened, brushing it off as being 'a little hospice humor.' A good sense of humor is critical to the emotional health and well-being of almost all medical professionals, and none more so than in the case of those who deal with death and dying every single day.

Unfortunately, not all calls for help contained such moments of levity with which to brighten up the darkness. One case involved a family who had been flagged as a possible problem because they were extremely emotional and upset about the inevitable passing of their mother, so much so that Robbin and her superiors felt that they might behave in a dangerously unpredictable manner once they heard that she had finally died.

Before venturing over to visit the patient at home, she phoned the on-call social worker and asked her to meet her over there. The two ladies arrived at the same time, and after ringing the doorbell were led downstairs by a member of the patient's family.

"We've already said our goodbyes," a man said as he passed them on the stairs.

The basement seemed to have been pulling double duty as a bedroom/living room for the dying woman. A large bed dominated one corner. Behind it was a tall standing lamp, about as big as an average adult, with a single dim bulb. It was the only source of light in the very gloomy downstairs room.

Chairs had been set up all around the bed in a semi-circle, a sign that the family had spent time congregating around their mother as she spent her last few hours among the living. The old lady herself was lying in the bed with a sheet pulled up and over her head. No strangers to the world of death and dying, Robbin and the social worker nevertheless found the sight of the covered corpse to be more than a little creepy.

Despite what you may have seen on TV or in the movies, most medical professionals don't close the eyes of a dead person or cover them up with a sheet — it tends to annoy the coroner's staff, for one thing, who prefer a death scene to remain as undisturbed as possible when it comes time to carry out an investigation, if one is needed. But over the course of her many years spent certifying in-home deaths, Robbin had found that this was a fairly common trend. Family members seemed to feel compelled to dim the lights and to cover up the face of their loved one once they had taken their last breath.

In this particular case, there was no need for an autopsy. The patient had been ill for a long time, and the death had been expected, the natural endpoint of a long life that had been very well lived, if the size of her family was any guide.

Slowly, with the utmost respect and care, Robbin reached out and grasped the hem of the sheet, pulling it slowly back to uncover the dead woman's face. She was most definitely gone. The lined features, which must once have smiled, frowned, and seen countless different expressions over the course of her long lifetime, were now completely slack and immobile. There is a unique stillness that accompanies physical death, one which is quite unmistakable to those who have encountered it. Robbin knew with absolute certainty that her charge really was dead.

Nevertheless, as a nurse, she still had a job to do. Once she had verified the state of clinical death by checking with her stethoscope, Robbin gently covered the dead woman's face with the sheet once more, then she and the social worker sat down in the vacant seats that surrounded the bed. They talked in low, hushed tones, dealing with the host of administrative minutiae that accompanied every in-home death. Had a funeral home been selected, and were they expecting a phone call to come and pick up the body? Was the paperwork filled out and ready to be submitted? In modern-day society, dying can be every bit as complex (and expensive) as living can be.

Looking back on the events of that night all these years later, Robbin reflects on what she describes as a kind of 'special sense' that nurses have.

"We nurses all talk about having it. When you walk in to pronounce a patient, you can tell if they're still there or not. There's often a strong feeling of them either being right there in the room with you, usually in or around the body, or of that body being nothing more than an empty husk."

She describes it as being a totally different feeling in each case. This isn't necessarily a psychic sensation (though it could possibly be exactly that) but may well be a very finely-tuned way of subconsciously perceiving the local environment. After all, when a nurse works around death for a prolonged period of time, he or she soon comes to know its ways without ever consciously thinking about it. This may be a similar process to the way in which hunches and intuition work. Many nurses do seem to be remarkably empathic and intuitive than their fellow members of society by nature, particularly when it comes to their chosen field of endeavor – medicine.

Looking slowly around the shadowy room, Robbin could not shake the distinct impression that the patient was still there. Although her spirit, soul, call it what you will, had severed its tie to the physical body, it had not yet begun to move on from it.

Both women continued to talk quietly. They were sitting right next to the deceased woman, with a clear view of the bed and the shrouded body that lay upon it. Suddenly, without any sort of warning, what looked like a large soap bubble rose up from the center of her chest, directly above her diaphragm. Completely transparent, it glowed from within, illuminated by its own form of ethereal light.

Climbing slowly upward, the 'bubble' hovered a foot above the dead woman for a brief moment, before suddenly putting on a burst of speed and flying upward, disappearing through the ceiling above their heads.

Turning to face each other, the nurse and the social worker both said at exactly the same time: "Did you *see* that?!?!"

It was the only time that Robbin had ever seen something actually leaving the body after death, some tangible manifestation of what she firmly believed was the human soul, departing for realms unknown.

Almost immediately, Robbin could feel a difference in the atmosphere within that room. She could tell beyond all shadow of a doubt that the dead woman's spirit presence was no longer there.

All that remained was an empty shell.

CHAPTER THREE
Major Trauma

Robbin once worked as an emergency room nurse in a major hospital that has long since closed its doors. At the time she worked there, the hospital was an extremely old one, with a lot of history in its walls. Needless to say, it had a reputation among the employees for being haunted, and many strange things took place there day in, day out.

Many of the nurses and support staff heard whispers coming from empty rooms, particularly at night, along with the sound of the curtains which surrounded each of the E.R. beds swishing back and forth on their own.

Shadow figures were spotted moving about the place, seeming to play hide-and-go-seek with the care providers who looked after the patients there.

On one particular night, there was a huge motor vehicle accident — multiple cars had plowed into one another at high speed. Such incidents often have very high casualty rates. Broken bones, internal bleeding, and even blunt force cardiac arrests are not uncommon, and the paramedics and EMTs who attend upon such calls usually have their hands full.

As a matter of course, trauma surgeons will come downstairs to meet their prospective patients in the emergency room itself, in order to gauge the severity of their injuries and perform a few initial life-saving treatments that will stabilize the victim, before taking them up to the operating room for surgery.

Robbin was assigned to assist one of the surgeons. It wasn't long before the first ambulances began to arrive, the paramedics throwing the doors open wide and wheeling their critically injured patients through into the emergency room. Nurses separated them out and directed each one into a specific trauma bay, what those in the emergency medical field like to call 'the big room.'

The big room is the part of the hospital where the first part of the battle between life and death takes place.

Doctors, nurses, and all manner of technicians descend upon the patient from all sides. Breathing tubes are inserted into airways; additional IVs are started; long, thick needles are pushed deep into the chest in order to release air under pressure and allow the wounded person to begin to breathe again. These and a host of other procedures all need to happen in the space of just a few minutes. Time is precious; every second counts, and the seasoned trauma specialists know it.

Robbin and her colleagues had done this many times before, and were very good at what they did. They *had* to be, because the patient that had been entrusted into their care was in a very bad way indeed. His neck was broken, and had to be stabilized as quickly as possible. The man was drenched in blood — just how much of it was his own and how much was somebody else's wasn't immediately clear — and absolutely reeked of alcohol.

Go to an emergency department in practically any American hospital on a Friday or Saturday night, and you will discover that roughly half of the patients are there for reasons that have something to do with alcohol. This includes those poor innocent souls who were, through no fault of their own, unfortunate enough to be struck by a drunk driver, or find themselves punched in the face by somebody who has had too much to drink in a bar.

For Robbin and her colleagues in the emergency room, this was just another night on the job…

…but for the trauma surgeon, it had just undergone a very ugly twist.

The patient was struggling, fighting the trauma team with his fists and feet.

"Stop it," the trauma surgeon screamed, slamming the patient back down on the bed. *"STOP FUCKING AROUND!"*

The injured, halfway-delirious man took no notice, so the surgeon lunged up onto the bed and stuck a knee in his chest, seemingly heedless of the patient's wounds. Robbin looked at him aghast. Yes, the patient had to be controlled, but this was crossing a line. She had worked with the same surgeon many times before, and knew him to be a calm man, the sort of quiet professional that was well-suited to his chosen vocation. Why had he suddenly lost control of himself like that? Something plainly wasn't right.

Nevertheless, his enraged body slam was effective, subduing the thrashing patient long enough for the trauma team to put him in restraints, Velcro straps around his wrists and ankles that greatly restricted his range of motion. Now they could finally do their jobs.

Once the patient was stabilized, his bed was wheeled up to the Intensive Care Unit (ICU), where the surgeon could scrub in and begin to definitively address his injuries. A police officer had been standing guard outside the trauma bay ever since the patient had first arrived. He accompanied the team up to the ICU, knowing that the patient —

assuming that he survived — was going to be arrested for DUI (Driving Under the Influence).

The big room looked like an abattoir, the tile floor covered with blood. Blood-soaked gauze bandages littered the room, along with the disposable paraphernalia that was used and then discarded whenever a critically-injured patient came in. The emergency room technicians and nurses set about cleaning it up.

Later that night, Robbin was sitting at the nurses' station, enjoying a well-earned cup of coffee with one of her colleagues. They began discussing the trauma surgeon's strange behavior.

"He was so aggressive, it took me by surprise," Robbin said, shaking her head. "That was totally out of character for him."

The other nurse cocked an eyebrow. "Didn't you hear?" he asked. "The doc had just pronounced two kids and both of their parents dead. Your patient was driving the car that killed them."

Robbin suddenly felt sick to her stomach. Four dead innocents, and she had been working on the man who had, for all intents and purposes, murdered them.

In a way, she was glad that she *hadn't* known. Not that it

would have affected the standard of her patient care one bit — like most nurses, she prided herself on doing a good job, no matter *who* her patient happened to be — but it would certainly have been an unwelcome distraction, as it had apparently been for the trauma surgeon. Seen in that light, now his aggressive behavior began to make a lot more sense.

"You know what I don't get?" the other nurse asked rhetorically. "Who was that other guy, standing at the back of the room?

"What other guy?" Robbin frowned. She didn't know who he was talking about. She hadn't seen anybody else in the room.

"He was standing in the far corner, just watching. I figured he was either a family member or a detective. The cop must have been okay with him being in there, so I had no problem with it."

Robbin had seen the room clearly, and could say with confidence that at no time had there been anybody in there that wasn't a part of the trauma team. But the other nurse stuck to his guns, adamant that he had seen this man. He went on to describe him down to the smallest detail, saying that he had been wearing a white shirt and glasses. More interesting still, when she asked around afterwards, Robbin discovered that some of the medical staff had seen the man and some of them hadn't; a couple even described him as having had blood on his face, as though he had sustained recent injuries.

Intrigued now, Robbin began to dig a little deeper. What she found out was incredible. The description of the quiet man in the corner of the room matched that of the deceased father that the trauma surgeon had pronounced dead just a few minutes before, right down the white shirt, glasses…and a blood-stained face.

One of the many intriguing facets of this case is why some members of the trauma team reported seeing the phantom visitor, and others hadn't the slightest idea that he was there.

Discounting the notion that this was a living human being right off the bat (how did he get past the cop guarding the doors?) means that the man had to be one of two things: either he was a hallucination, or he was an apparition.

The possibility of his having been a hallucination may seem to make sense at first glance. After all, some people are known to see things when they are stressed out. But this generally doesn't happen with experienced medical resuscitation teams. Working in high-stress, life or death circumstances is their bread and butter, and it takes a lot to freak them out, generally speaking.

If the man *was* a hallucination, then he would have to have been some form of *mass* hallucination, because multiple members of the resuscitation team saw him, and described him in exactly the same way, nailing his clothing and activities (restricted to simply standing there quietly and observing) to a 'T.'

It seems far more likely that the departing spirit of the deceased father had stopped in to witness the team attempt to resuscitate the man who had taken his life, and that of his family.

One suspects that he wasn't rooting too hard for their success.

CHAPTER FOUR
Help Me Breathe

Of the many afflictions from which a person may suffer in their later years, Chronic Obstructive Pulmonary Disease is one of the most uncomfortable. It is usually, though not always, the end results of years, if not decades spent smoking. The pollutants and toxins contained in cigarette smoke slowly eat away at the tissue of the lungs, breaking them down and seriously degrading the sufferer's ability to breathe.

As the condition progresses and the lungs continue to rot, the COPDer (as many medical professionals refer to them) undergoes the very unpleasant experience of being unable to catch their breath even when they are at rest.

Imagine, if you will, that a healthy lung looks something like a sponge, interspersed with lots of small holes. The lungs of a person suffering from COPD have many more holes, and those holes are much bigger, which means that the lungs tend to trap de-oxygenated air in the dead spaces, preventing them from breathing out effectively.

Such patients are forced to rely on supplemental oxygen throughout the day. As their health worsens, they are dependent on nasal cannulas and face masks to deliver a constant flow of life-giving oxygen; even then, it is often a struggle for them to draw breath. They are slowly suffocating. COPD is an irreversible disease, one that can never be cured, and causes many thousands of deaths each year.

As the condition reaches its more advanced stages, the patients require constant care and support. Many live out their last days in nursing homes and residential facilities. Such was the case with Randall (not his real name), a life-long smoker. Reaching the end of a long life, he had little lung capacity left any more. Unable to move, the poor man was now completely bed-ridden, totally reliant on the nurses and aides to take care of him.

The entirety of Randall's days and nights consisted of nothing more than fighting to breathe. Day in, day out, he would lay there in bed, propped up on a big stack of pillows, wheezing and gasping into an oxygen mask.

"Help me. Please help me," he would beg, pleading for something, for *anything* to give him respite.

Anney was one of the nurses who was charged to look after Randall. Other than give him oxygen and the medications prescribed to him, she could do very little else to make him more comfortable.

Just like most health care providers, Anney had a big, compassionate heart. The sound of Randall's torment was almost too much for her to bear.

As the days dragged on into weeks, Randall's condition worsened. Finally, the inevitable happened — Randall's heart gave out, and he died. Anney and her fellow care providers were saddened by his loss, but at the same time, very much relieved that he was now free from all pain and suffering.

You don't work in the field of health care without getting somewhat acquainted with death. Patients die; it is the sad reality that there are some conditions which simply cannot be cured, even with the many great advances in medicine that science has brought. Medical professionals grow certain emotional calluses; if they didn't, it would be impossible for them to stay sane. The constant stress and grief would simply be too overwhelming.

Randall's body was taken away, his personal effects were given to his next of kin, and his room was cleaned and prepared for a future resident. Life in the nursing home went on as usual.

A few weeks after Randall's death, Anney and two of

her colleagues were sitting at the nurse's station, discussing their plans for the approaching shift. It was the middle of the day, and they had a lot to get done before the night shift started.

Suddenly, they heard a sound from the end of the hallway that stopped their conversation cold.

"Did you hear that?" asked one of the nurses, her tone full of disbelief. "It sounded like…"

"It can't have been," Anney said.

But it was. After just a few seconds, they heard the sound again. It was a voice, one that they all knew well; a wheezing, raspy voice, full of fear and distress.

"Help me," it gasped. *"Please help me…"*

"That's coming from Randall's room," Anney said.

The three nurses just looked at one another. Their first thought was that it was just a little before one o'clock in the afternoon, which meant that almost all of the residents would be up and about. Surely the voice must have come from one of them?

But then Anney pointed out that they were all eating their lunch in the dining hall. Besides, that voice had been a little too familiar to have belonged to somebody other than…

"Randall?" she said, making her way tentatively down

the hall toward his former room. The two other nurses followed her.

"Help me...Please, help me..."

Every room that they passed along the way was empty. That entire wing of the nursing home was deserted. But somebody was speaking.

"Please help me..." The wheezing was painful to listen to, the sound of ravaged lungs fighting desperately to move air.

Anney reached the door to what had until just a few weeks before been Randall's room. Somebody else called it home now. When she and her two colleagues went inside, they found it to be empty.

The man's voice had stopped speaking. The three nurses stood in the center of the room. The only sound they could hear was the pounding of their own hearts and their regular, measured breathing

Breathing…

"Randall, was that you?" Anney asked. She felt slightly foolish, talking to thin air like that, but they all knew what they had heard. It had been Randall's voice. They were certain of it. "Were you asking for help?"

No answer came.

"We miss you, Randall," one of the other nurses said. "But you don't have to be afraid any more. The pain is gone. You can breathe again, if you need to. Everything is going to be okay."

Anney kept expecting Randall to answer them, but he never did. "You don't have to stay here, Randall," she told the dead man. "You can move on. There is help available to you, if you want it. All you have to do is ask."

The trio of nurses stood there in silence for a few more minutes. One by one, the nursing home residents began to trickle back from lunch, making their way back to their rooms. The gentleman who now called Randall's room home didn't ask what they were doing in there, and none of them volunteered that information, figuring that if Randall was still hanging around, then he would make for a harmless invisible room-mate.

After they had reassured him that everything was going to be okay, that his pain and suffering were over, Randall's voice was never heard again.

CHAPTER FIVE
The Tunnels

One of the things I discovered when I was researching my book *The World's Most Haunted Hospitals* is just how difficult it can be to get healthcare workers to talk about their paranormal experiences on the record.

It's easy to understand why that would be the case. Most hospital administrators take a very dim view of their employees telling ghost stories at work. Hospitals and nursing homes are supposed to be places of peace, security and healing, where the sick can get better and those who need special care and attention can have their needs met. Stories of shadow figures, poltergeist activity, and things that go bump in the night are definitely not conducive to any of that.

You don't have to look very far to find healthcare workers who have been fired, or at the very least had their career prospects cut short, because they have spoken openly about a ghostly experience that happened to them while they were working.

Some people choose to speak out regardless, making no efforts whatsoever to hide their interest in things that go bump in the night. I'm one of them — having written quite a few books on the subject of ghosts and hauntings, and appearing in several TV shows means that my cover was blown a long time ago — and so is Anney, a nurse who makes no secret of her fascination for all things paranormal.

Most of the other medical staff who worked in the same hospital were aware of Anney's interest, and made sure to send any ghost stories that they heard her way. In fact, the night security guards found some of the haunted areas to be so frightening that they always called her and asked her to escort them whenever they needed to go and check something out there.

Anney worked primarily on the second floor, not too far away from the pediatric ward, which is why she began to hear stories about the ghost of a little boy who was said to haunt the place.

The phantom had developed a reputation for visiting some of the patients during the night, tucking them into bed as they were drifting off to sleep, or covering them up when they were getting cold.

On one particular evening, the duty nurse looked up from her charting to see that one of the patient call lights was flashing. When she went to find out what was the matter, the wide-eyed patient told her that she had seen the apparition of a little boy walk into the closet in her room.

As an avowed believer in ghosts and spirits, Anney didn't often feel the need to take such stories with a grain of salt. Late one night, one of her own patients pushed their call button. "I'm cold," the patient complained, and so Anney went to fetch her a warm blanket from the linen closet.

It took her less than three minutes. When she returned, Anney was surprised to find that her patient was already covered up with a blanket. "That sweet little boy brought it for me," she explained, not thinking to ask why a child would be up so late, much less be fetching blankets for complete strangers in a hospital.

Anney didn't need to ask any more about it. She already knew the answer, especially as she was working on the south side, where appearances of the ghost child were most often reported.

The following night, she was working in the same spot. Another call light, but this time it was a complaint, rather than a request: "Nurse, could you please do something about the young man who keeps going in and out of the closet? It's preventing me from falling asleep!"

As with many larger towns, the one in which Anney

worked was served by not just one but two hospitals. When one of them closed down, many of the staff came to work at the same hospital as she did. The now-defunct facility had once been a Catholic hospital, which went some way toward explaining why the new employees told stories of a phantom nun haunting the place.

Many hospitals used to be staffed primarily by nuns, and these ladies of faith are still a fixture of some hospitals today (when I was undergoing training at a Catholic hospital's paramedic academy in 2009, nuns were a part of the staff).

There was an impressive consistency to the stories being told about this particular spirit. Clad from head to toe in a white habit, the ghostly nun was usually seen walking through the hospital wards. Whenever a nurse caught sight of the nun, they would always follow her to see where she was going — her destination was usually the room of a patient. When the nurse reached the room and went inside, the patient was found to have already passed away, which meant that the nun was a harbinger of death.

Although the hospital itself was closed down, the psychiatric ward and rehabilitation unit both remained open. This meant that a security guard had to be kept on staff, and it just so happened that he was a friend of Anney's. She managed to talk him into giving her a tour of the underground tunnels that connected the hospital building with the nunnery. A Certified Nursing Assistant (CNA) from the psychiatric unit came along with them.

The tunnels were dark and creepy, which was only to be expected. Anney and her two companions made their way slowly toward the abandoned hospital, they suddenly felt an invisible pair of hands grab them by the arms.

Before they could say anything more than, "What the hell...?" they found themselves being forcibly turned around and pushed back in the direction from which they had come. Something most definitely did not want the three of them to be down there, and was making that known in no uncertain terms.

The grip had been extremely firm, so tight that when Anney rolled up her sleeves afterward, her upper arms were encircled with a pair of angry red bruises.

After that, she refused to ever go back into the haunted tunnels.

I find it hard to blame her for that – I mean, would *you* have gone back...?

CHAPTER SIX
A Last Goodbye

Of the many different sub-disciplines that comprise the nursing profession, few are more challenging than that of the Intensive Care Unit. This is where many seriously ill, often close-to-death patients can be found. It is a highly technical, high-stakes arena of medical care that is most definitely not for the faint of heart.

For some patients, it is the last place that they will ever see in this life.

One such patient, an elderly gentleman, was well-known to Anney. He was a frequent visitor to the ICU, and as his health slowly deteriorated, the poor man entered a downward spiral from which he would sadly never recover.

The man desperately needed cardiac catheterization, a procedure in which a small wire is snaked through an artery in the groin or thigh all the way up into the coronary arteries, where it allows a skilled cardiologist to clear blockages that are impeding blood flow to the heart.

Anney knew that without the life-saving intervention, her patient would almost certainly die. Although nurses aren't supposed to have favorite patients, this kind, funny, and charming man had nevertheless become just that. She therefore used every ounce of reason and rational argument in trying to talk him into undergoing the procedure, yet no matter how much she ultimately begged and pleaded, the old man adamantly refused to give permission.

It was not hard for her to understand why. She only had to look at him. Tubes, wires, and all manner of medical paraphernalia were hooked up to his body. Monitors beeped and chimed rhythmically. He was getting more medications each day than most patients received in a year.

"I'm sick of all this," he told her, "Just sick and tired of it all. I want it to be over and done with."

Looking at it from her patient's point of view, Anney could see why he didn't want to spend the rest of what little life he had getting poked with needles and undergoing other uncomfortable, sometimes painful treatments. She chose her next question with great care.

"If your heart stops, do you want us to try and resuscitate you?"

"I don't care," he said stubbornly.

Patients who didn't want the ICU staff to try and bring them back if their heart gave out were required to sign a form known as a DNR (Do Not Resuscitate) order, a legal document which basically allows them to die naturally without the nurses and doctors intervening.

Before the issue of getting him a DNR could be settled, a strident, monotone beeping noise told Anney that her patient had just gone into cardiac arrest.

Immediately, she called a code. Help came running, bringing the crash cart with them. Resuscitation is an intricately-choreographed dance, and ICU team members are masters in their field. One nurse immediately began CPR, pushing on the old man's chest in order to keep his blood circulating throughout his body, maintaining the flow of life-saving oxygen to his brain and other vital organs. Another began to administer epinephrine, intended to kick-start the heart and try to raise the blood pressure, while a third worked on managing the airway.

Anney now found herself in a tough spot. She knew that the old gentleman didn't want to be resuscitated — he had made that very clear to her — but without a signed document to protect them, the hospital team had potentially opened themselves up to great liability if her patient's family objected to them allowing him to die. That was why she had had no option but to begin the resuscitation process…but she didn't want to continue it for a second longer than was necessary. CPR is not a gentle thing; more often than not, the cartilage which connects the ribs to the breastbone cracks and shatters under the force of the compressions. Although the patient feels nothing, the thought of such an act being carried out with no real chance of the patient ever surviving to live a meaningful life is one which does not sit well with many health care providers.

Nevertheless, their efforts worked. The old man's pulse returned. Although he was no longer conscious, the ICU team had managed to restore a heartbeat. It was weak, thready, and erratic…but it was still a heartbeat.

Wanting a clear sense of direction, she phoned the man's next of kin, which happened to be his brother. Explaining everything clearly and in as much detail as she could, Anney told the man that his brother did not have long to live. His reprieve was temporary, due mostly to the medications that they had given him, and his weakened heart would not cling to life for much longer. What did he want them to do?

Suddenly, just as she was speaking mid-sentence, she felt her head jerked backward sharply, startling her. Something had grabbed her ponytail and pulled it, hard. At first she thought that somebody had picked the most inappropriate time imaginable to play a practical joke on her.

Swinging around, she opened her mouth to give the culprit a piece of her mind — and stopped, her jaw agape.

Standing there in the hospital corridor was her patient. Although he was still wearing his backless gown, the IVs, tubes, and electrodes were all gone. They looked at one another in silence for a moment. Stunned, Anney was unable to speak. The old man simply shook his head at her, mutely telling her, *No.*

From inside the patient's room, the cardiac monitor flatlined once more. His heart had stopped for a second time. Annie couldn't hear it, as the door was closed, but she knew beyond all shadow of a doubt what had just happened.

She continued to stare at her patient, receiving his message loud and clear. *Please don't put me through any more of this*, he seemed to be saying, his eyes desperately pleading with her.

"PLEASE keep him alive until I can get there to say goodbye," her patient's brother begged Anney.

"I have to go," she said, hanging up and stepping back into the patient's room. "He's back in cardiac arrest," she announced, a statement of fact rather than a question.

"How did you know that?" asked the attending physician, obviously puzzled.

Without thinking, Anney replied that the patient had just told her so himself. Everybody in the room turned to stare at her. She could not have gotten stranger looks if she had suddenly sprouted a second head.

"He pulled my hair," she said, "and he wants you to stop working on him."

Standing on the other side of the bed, behind his own physical body, was the apparition of Anney's patient. Now he was nodding, pleased that his message had been received and understood.

But the resuscitation process continued. Seeing that everything that medically needed to happen was already being done, she slipped around to the opposite side of the bed. Bending over the unconscious patient's physical form, she spoke in a low whisper, explaining to the man that it was his brother's heartfelt wish for them to keep him alive — no, she corrected, to keep his *body* alive — until he could arrive for a final goodbye.

"Can you hang in there for just a little longer?" Anney asked. "So that your brother can see you one last time?"

Incredibly, the patient nodded, a single, almost spastic jerk of the head. Was this simply a side-effect of the resuscitation process, Anney wondered, or had he just told her that he would try his best for his brother's sake?

Either way, despite having gone into cardiac arrest multiple times, the tenacious old gentleman did indeed hang on to life until the following morning, when his brother made it to his bedside to say his last goodbyes. With his brother clutching his hand and Annie embracing him, the patient passed away three minutes later, leaving this life with what almost sounded like a contented sigh.

CHAPTER SEVEN
Graveyard Nightmares

During my twenty-five years as a paranormal investigator, I have come across many different types of haunted location — everything from prisons, offices, and ships, to battlefields, crime scenes, and (in one particularly memorable instance) the home of a serial killer.

As was mentioned earlier, a disproportionate number of hauntings seem to take place in medical facilities of one sort or another, whether they are hospitals, sanatoriums, psychiatric facilities, or nursing homes. No matter what type and quality of care these facilities provide, they all share one thing in common: for the most part, their owners and administrators usually shun the negative publicity which can come along with reported sightings of ghosts and other paranormal activity.

Sometimes, the inhabitants of such facilities can be more terrifying than anything ghostly could ever be. A case in point comes to us from a nurse named Susan, a home health aide and CNA (Certified Nursing Assistant) who worked in a residential care facility.

This nursing home had a reputation for being haunted,

with multiple eyewitnesses encountering the apparition of a man wearing a cowboy hat. This particular ghost liked to keep himself to himself, and whenever he was seen, he was simply hanging out at the end of one specific hallway, simply minding his own business. Despite the prevalence of the ghost sightings, Susan had never seen him herself. She worked the graveyard shift, from 11pm to 7am, when the nursing home was at its most quiet, and she did not find the idea of a 'phantom cowboy' to be even remotely frightening, but the same could not be said for two of the residents

Due to his failing health, one of the residents was brought to the nursing home from a state-level facility. He had been institutionalized for many years, having been diagnosed as being clinically insane. Susan made a point of not enquiring too closely about his crimes, because she found the man himself to be quite frightening enough. All of the staff were afraid of this man, due to his habit of glowering malevolently at them whenever they were around him. He communicated in a series of guttural grunts and barks that were more animalistic than human.

Whenever Susan or any of her colleagues were in his room, attempting to take care of him, the patient tended to become physically violent, trying to lash out with his feet and fists, or more worrisome still, biting at them whenever they got too close.

Susan came to believe that the patient wasn't simply criminally insane; rather, she was convinced that some kind of spirit had taken him over. Something dark and inhuman.

When the man laughed, what came from his throat wasn't the sort of laugh that came from a human voice box. This was something altogether different, more feral and bestial — the sort of harsh glottic sound that would issue from the mouth of a creature.

So aggressive was the patient, in fact, that he was never permitted to have a room-mate, no matter how short on space the facility was. He was simply too wild and out of control. The more she came to know the man, the more convinced she was that he was possessed by some kind of malevolent entity. One is forced to wonder whether, if this was indeed the case, it had played a hand in whatever crimes the patient had been institutionalized for having committed.

On the other hand, it is equally possible that the patient was simply just what he appeared to be — insane. Sometimes, those who are deeply mentally and emotionally disturbed present as if they are some kind of beast or monster, and can be extremely frightening for care providers to be faced with. In the case of this particular patient, despite Susan's conviction, it is impossible to say for sure either way.

While it is convenient (and often correct) to dismiss patients such as this as being mentally ill, there are some instances in which that explanation does not cover all of the bases. Take, for example, another patient that Susan cared for, a lady in her mid-fifties. She was in such poor health that she was bedridden, unable to get up and about during the daytime, and sadly didn't have much of a life beyond the confines of the four walls of her room. Unfortunately, she had no close family and next to no visitors either.

This particular lady had three room-mates, sharing a spacious room with each of them taking one corner for themselves. When darkness fell, things got to be very bad. She had a tendency to yell and scream at the staff and fellow patients alike, glaring and making physical threats. Her behavior became much more severe at night.

One evening, Susan, a fellow CNA, and a nurse were all attempting to render care. The patient was having none of it, thrashing and shrieking as though possessed.

"There's somebody outside!" the old woman screamed at the top of her lungs. Despite the best efforts of Susan and her colleagues to reassure her, she continued to yell about there being a person right standing outside the window. In an attempt to mollify her, Susan pulled back the curtain to prove that there was nobody outside. There were no footsteps in the fresh carpet of snow that blanketed the ground either.

The patient was not reassured. If anything, she became even more hysterical, screaming and growling at the three healthcare providers. Susan stepped outside her room, pulling the door shut. More than a little unnerved, she began to whisper the Lord's Prayer. Suddenly, from behind the closed door, she heard the same words being repeated back a half-second after she said them, in a voice that was mocking and full of spite.

Somehow, the patient was able to hear her, and was taunting Susan by throwing her own words back at her. Stepping back into the patient's room, Susan approached her bed. The lights began to flicker off and on — not necessarily unusual on a cold winter's night, except for the fact that the power brownout was isolated to just this one room. The lights in the hallway and other parts of the nursing home were unaffected, making it a strangely specific phenomenon.

Then the temperature in the room began to drop. The

nurse and both CNAs agreed that it was noticeably colder. The patient seemed unaffected, and simply continued to rock back and forth in bed, throwing spiteful comments at the three women and insisting that somebody was standing outside her window.

This continued throughout the night, until finally, exhausted, she drifted off to sleep.

Susan and her colleagues were unable to explain the strange events of that night, and to this day are uncertain whether they were paranormal in nature or simply a series of very strange coincidences.

In the case of the second patient, one of the first things that comes to mind is Sundowner Syndrome. This is a condition which affects roughly twenty percent of the five million Americans who suffer with Alzheimer's. The classic presentation of Sundowner Syndrome is the dementia patient who becomes increasingly unstable at night, threatening, screaming, and often physically abusing their fellow patients and caregivers.

Sundowner Syndrome takes an already cruel disease and makes it even worse for all concerned, particularly the family members of the afflicted sufferer.

While the patient described by Susan does at first seem like a good fit for this particular malady, it must be pointed out that Sundowners Syndrome in no way explains the physical phenomena that Susan reported.

—How did she hear through the door?
—Was the power brownout a coincidence?
—What caused the temperature drop?

Many things that were once believed to be supernatural in nature have now been satisfactorily explained by science.

One example is the full-body tonic-clonic seizure, a series of violent jerks and convulsions. Once believed to be a sign of demonic possession, we now know it for what it really is: the random firings of chaotic nervous impulses deep inside the brain. We can also treat it with medications.

Yet there are still those patients whose presentations seem to defy medical explanation. There is a tendency for doctors to write them off under the catch-all umbrella of 'mental illness,' yet as I talk to those fellow medical professionals who also have an interest in the paranormal, something interesting emerges. More and more of them are coming to believe that other factors – perhaps we should say other *forces* – may be at work.

Some believe in the possibility of possession. Others believe in the existence of spiritual attachments, a sort of 'psychic hitch-hiker' that is capable of latching onto an unsuspecting victim and influencing their behavior and emotional state to suit its own ends.

Clearly, more research needs to be done in this area. As the medical community is unlikely to go near such a subject with a ten-foot barge pole (to do so would be the equivalent of career suicide for a physician) then it is once again left up to the paranormal investigator to carry out research, then share his or her own data and conclusions with the rest of us.

This is a fascinating fringe aspect of paranormal research that raises more questions than it answers…

…for now.

CHAPTER EIGHT
The Seventh Floor

Over the long course of her medical career as a paramedic, Trish thought that she had seen it all.

Responding to shootings, stabbings, and all manner of death, illness, and injury sometimes gives one a somewhat jaded view of life. We tend to think we've seen it all. But then, every so often, something happens which reminds us of just how untrue that can be.

One such experience happened to Trish back in 1991.

The hospital had a reputation for being haunted. A lot of the employees — especially those who worked during the daytime — just shrugged it off, dismissing the ghost stories and going about their everyday business.

The night shift workers, on the other hand, were a different matter entirely. It seemed that practically every nurse who worked late there avoided the seventh floor like the plague. Patients were no longer placed on that floor, as there were issues with the electrical wiring, and it was said to be extremely haunted.

Being a salty-as-hell EMT with a side interest in all things paranormal, Trish naturally wanted to go up there and check it out for herself. Unfortunately, that was a no-go; as a safety measure, the elevator had been programmed not to stop at the seventh floor, and she didn't particularly feel like climbing seven flights of stairs at the end of her long shift.

One night, Trish and her partner were finishing up an inter-facility transfer, which usually involves taking a patient from one hospital or nursing home to another. They had dropped the patient off on one of the upper floors, turning patient care over to the on-duty nurse, and wheeled their stretcher to the elevator for the return trip.

Trish hit the button for the ground floor. The elevator began to descend. She was lost in her own thoughts, hoping that the rest of her shift would be a quiet one, when the elevator car suddenly stopped…

…on the seventh.

"Oh, crap," she whispered. Suddenly, her desire to delve into the mysteries of the haunted floor wasn't as strong as it had been just a few minutes before.

The elevator doors opened onto a long hallway that was completely black. Two rows of open doors stretched away into the distance, disappearing into the gloom.

The two EMTs stood there in silence for a moment, just starring out into the darkness.

"What do you want to do?" Trish's partner broke the silence with a hushed whisper.

Wordlessly, Trish stepped off the elevator, wheeling the stretcher along with her. Putting on the brake to prevent it from rolling off, the two EMTs set out to explore the haunted floor, breaking out their flashlights to help them navigate.

Their first stop was the nurse's station, long since abandoned, save for a few scattered sheets of paper.

"HELLLLLOOOOOO!" Trish called out. "Is there anybody there?"

There was no answer. The EMTs decided to explore, prowling the hallways. Each patient room that they passed had a fully made-up bed, the crisp white sheets coated in a thick layer of dust.

The atmosphere felt heavy and oppressive. Trish was unable to shake the distinct feeling that she was being followed, though whenever she turned to look over her shoulder, there was never a soul to be seen.

A sudden voice, loud and scratchy, made the two EMTs jump halfway out of their skin. Trish's heart rate doubled in the space of a few seconds, pounding hard in her chest. Fortunately, there was a very simple explanation: dispatch was calling them over the radio, checking in on their whereabouts and making sure that they were okay.

Telling the dispatcher that everything was just fine and they would be clearing the hospital and returning to service shortly, she let out a long, slow breath. The unexpected radio call had startled her.

Tempting fate, her partner called out, "There's no such thing as ghosts!"

Big mistake.

As if in direct answer to her ill-chosen words, a blast of icy-cold air suddenly gusted past them, making both of them shriek in fear. Each and every one of the doors on either side of the hallway slammed shut, the dull thud almost deafening. Trish and her partner screamed again, all thoughts of further exploration now gone. They turned and bolted for the elevator, making to drag the stretcher inside without bothering to kick the brake off first…

…except the doors wouldn't open. Just as they had been warned, the seventh floor elevator call button had been disabled.

They were stuck up there.

Trish tried to call out on her radio, but all she could get was static. Desperately, she tried to think of a solution. Cell phones weren't around back then, and with the walkie-talkie not working, that only left a land-line.

Suddenly, she remembered seeing a phone back at the nurse's station.

To get to it, all she had to do was run the gauntlet of doors. Trish decided right there and then that if the doors all spontaneously opened themselves, there was a very real chance that she might need to change her underwear before the night was over.

Fortunately for Trish and her partner, the journey to the nurse's station was uneventful, even if it did seem to take an age to get there. Finally, picking up the phone, she dialed security and explained her plight.

Moments later, the elevator pinged and the doors opened. A security guard emerged, looking less than thrilled to be called away from whatever he'd been doing in order to fetch two wayward EMTs who had gotten themselves trapped.

The guard beckoned them into the elevator. Trish and her partner managed to somehow squeeze themselves and the stretcher in there. Taking note of their pale faces and generally frazzled appearance, he simply shook his head and chuckled.

"Somebody should have warned you both. The ghosts up

there on the seventh just *love* messing around with the newbies…"

Another day, another inter-facility transfer for Trish, now a paramedic, and her EMT partner. Such calls are the bread and butter of most private ambulance systems, and while transfers have none of the glamor of 911 emergency responses, they are every bit as important in the grand scheme of things. This is how patients are taken to new homes, loved ones are reunited, and those who are truly sick are taken to a higher level of care and treatment.

Inter-facility transfers often involve what EMS providers refer to as "the hospice run." Such calls are among the most important things that EMTs and paramedics can ever be called upon to do; it is a sacred thing to take a person on what will usually be their final ride ever. It is not unknown for EMS crews to divert for a few moments to take a patient on an impromptu tour through the neighborhood in which they once grew up, or to sit quietly in some out-of-the-way place in order for the dying person to watch the last sunrise they will ever see.

On this particular day, Trish and her partner were

assigned to transport a patient from a big city hospital to a hospice facility. When she and her partner arrived, the patient's family were all gathered around the bedside of a sweet little 89 year-old lady. She took a moment to review the nurse's notes, and saw that her patient was dying of kidney failure and heart failure.

At such an advanced age, the vital organs simply begin to wear out, no matter how much care one has taken of them during their lifetime.

"She's been very quiet," the patient's daughter told Trish. "Mom really hasn't been talking very much."

The nurse hadn't given Trish's partner a DNR, which almost all hospice patients have. One by one, the family members took it in turn to say their last goodbye. Wanting to give them a little privacy and space, the EMTs waited outside the room. The plan was for their patient's children to meet them at the hospice.

Trish and her partner placed their patient carefully on the pram, taking care to jostle her as little as possible. When she was loaded in the back of the ambulance, Trish sat on the bench seat next to her, assuming the role of the attendant, while her partner drove. She liked to talk to her patients, even those who were unconscious or unable to hear her back; it was a simple, compassionate gesture, and sometimes the only thing that could be done for them.

"I'm just going to take your blood pressure," Trish said, wrapping the cuff around the old lady's upper arm and inflating it. She listened carefully over her elbow with her stethoscope. It came as no big surprise for her to discover that her patient's vital signs were very poor indeed. There wasn't much that could be done about it at this late stage, other than to keep her as comfortable as possible.

With her vitals recorded, there was little else for Trish to do but sit back and keep a watchful eye on her charge while the miles rolled by. Taking out her tablet, she began typing up her patient care report. With no treatments being administered, it wasn't going to be a very long narrative.

Every so often, Trish would look up and make sure that the woman was still breathing.

The old lady opened her eyes, offering Trish a feeble smile. After a moment, the EMT realized that rather than looking at her, the patient was staring off to the right of her, at an empty spot next to Trish on the bench seat.

"Frank is there," the patient said, her voice raspy and weak. "My husband Frank. He's riding with us…right there next to you."

Trish looked out of the corner of her eye, then slowly turned her head. She couldn't see anybody else in the back of the ambulance with them. Nevertheless, the hairs on the back of her neck and arms began to stand up.

She took the old lady's hand and gave it a reassuring squeeze, but her patient seemed oblivious to the kindly gesture; she had begun to carry on a one-sided conversation with thin air.

"How is Beth?" she asked, before waiting for an answer that only she could hear. More questions followed, with more silent answers. The old lady became increasingly animated. "I can't wait to see Beth again. We can go and see some new lighthouses!"

For her part, Trish simply smiled politely and continued to hold her hand.

"Oh, Frank...I lost my favorite sweater...you remember, the one that you bought for me...I just can't find it." She turned to look at Trish. "When we get there, could you be a dear and ask Ben to get me the white sweater — the one with the holly blossoms on the collar?"

"I sure will," Trish promised. "I'm sorry you lost it."

"That's okay. I think I know where it might be. Tell him to look in the closet. It's in the box that Andrea packed last week. That sweater is my favorite, you see, and Frank is telling me that he saw her put it there."

With that, the patient closed her eyes and began to snore gently. She drifted in and out of consciousness for the remainder of the drive.

Just as they had promised, her children were right there waiting for the ambulance when it arrived at the hospice. Assisted by some of the nursing staff, Trish and her partner gently transferred their patient over to the hospital bed…a bed that she was destined never to leave.

Once she was all tucked in, the old lady reached out and took Trish's hand. Beckoning her to lean in close, she whispered, "Skip is with you. He wants me to tell you that he is very, very proud of you, and that you really need to dust the Hummels."

Trish's eyes widened in shock. She didn't know what to say. Skip was the name of her adoptive grandfather. He had passed on eight years before, and had left her his collection of Hummel figurines after his death. She hadn't been doing a great job of dusting them.

"Th-thank you," Trish stammered, her eyes filling with tears. She smiled back at the old lady. Something indefinable passed between them, a shared understanding of the significance of this moment.

Stepping outside into the hallway, Trish approached the lady's family members and asked them who Ben was. A man stepped forward. "I'm Ben," he said quietly. "She's my mother."

Trish repeated her request concerning the white sweater, including all of the specific details. He turned a ghostly shade of pale. Turning toward one of the ladies who was present, he said, "Andrea, could you come over here for a second, please?"

Andrea was Ben's sister. He repeated the story, and asked Andrea if she had seen anything matching the description of his mother's sweater. It turned out that she had, and had packed it away in a box just the week before. Her story tracked exactly with what Ben's mother had told her.

"There's no way she could possibly have known that," Andrea said, obviously flustered. "I was all alone in her room when I packed the box away. Heck, I was all alone in the *house*. Nobody could have seen it."

But somebody *had* seen it: Frank. It transpired that Frank was Ben's father. He had died twenty-two years before, but apparently was keeping an eagle eye on his wife and family, especially now that his wife's end was drawing near.

"Forgive my curiosity," Trish began awkwardly, "But I have to ask…who's Beth, and what connection does she have with lighthouses?"

Ben blanched. "Beth was my younger sister. She died twenty years ago. During her lifetime, she had enjoyed exploring lighthouses with our family."

After she and her partner said their goodbyes, Trish couldn't get the day's events out of her mind for the next week or so. Several weeks later, Trish was running another inter-facility transfer call to the same hospice. As she walked past her former patient's room on the way back to her ambulance, she saw that somebody else was staying in there now.

As a rule, she never followed up on patients, but this time, something compelled her to ask after the old lady. As things turned out, she had passed away later that same night. She had died peacefully, wearing her favorite white sweater — the one with holly blossoms on the collar — and surrounded by all of her loved ones.

"I'm sure that she was holding hands with her Frank that very night," Trish reflects, "exploring new lighthouses with Beth…and who knows, maybe hanging out with my grandpa Skip…"

CHAPTER NINE
It's Only Natural to be Afraid

In addition to working in the healthcare field as a nurse, Amanda was a passionate paranormal investigator. She and her husband, Bill, had founded their own research society, and spent a lot of their spare time trying to unravel the mysteries of some of the most haunted locations in their native Australia.

On one particular day, Amanda was working in a nursing home, picking up an extra shift. The facility in question was not one of the nicer nursing homes out there — in fact, it was one of the worst that Amanda had ever seen. The floors were grimy, the carpets threadbare; an ever-present stench of stale urine pervaded the place.

More disconcerting than that, however, was the atmosphere, which she found to be thick and heavy, bordering on the oppressive. Although she couldn't quite put her finger on it, Amanda felt that there was just something about the nursing home that felt…*off* somehow.

Still, Amanda was a professional. She resolved to simply take care of her patients to the very best of her ability, and tried to shrug off the creepy feeling that seemed to grow ever stronger as the night wore on.

A second nurse accompanied Amanda on her rounds that evening. They didn't know one another very well, which made the first question that she asked Amanda sound a little unusual: "Do you believe in ghosts?"

Laughing, Amanda told her colleague about her background in paranormal investigation. For her part, the other nurse seemed relieved that Amanda wasn't laughing at her for her 'crazy beliefs.' It was a quiet night, and so she began to open up a little, telling Amanda about some of the ghostly encounters she had experienced at the nursing home.

The nurse saw some very strange things when she worked night shifts…such as the apparitions of former (now deceased) residents of the facility sitting in empty wheelchairs, or prowling around the shadowy hallways, walking through walls and closed doors as though they weren't even there.

As fantastic as such tales may seem to some, Amanda had no problem believing them. Nurses are very familiar with the many facets of death, and having worked in palliative care herself, she had garnered more than a few stories of her own. Besides, Amanda had psychic sensitivities of her own, and had seen more than her fair share of spirits in her time.

She soon had reasons of her own to believe that the nursing home was haunted. Walking up to find a picture that was hanging on the wall, now slowly spinning from left to right and back again, as though being turned by invisible hands, she knew that strange things were afoot. When Amanda approached the picture, it suddenly stopped moving.

Then there were the toilets that flushed themselves. After ruling out the obvious (none of them were fitted with automatic timers) Amanda could find no explanation for their odd behavior; neither could the plumber, who was left scratching his head in bemusement after tearing the toilet apart and putting it back together again several times, without finding any kind of mechanical fault whatsoever.

One of Amanda's regular in-hospital duties was that of caring for those patients who were actively dying, one of the most sacred aspects of a nurse's calling. To this day, she vividly recalls the circumstances surrounding a terminally-ill patient who was placed in her charge.

The poor man was in a great deal of pain and was quite understandably restless, unable to get settled or remain still for very long. The nurses had given him as much morphine as they could, in order to deal with the worst effects of the pain; if they could not take it away entirely, Amanda reasoned, they could at least blunt its sting as much as possible.

Knowing that his time to die was drawing near, she made a point of sitting at her patient's bedside. Nobody should ever have to depart from this life alone, and Amanda was determined to keep him company when he did finally pass.

As her patient squirmed restlessly in his bed, Amanda took his hand and gently asked him what was the matter. He raised one arm and shakily pointed to an empty chair on the far side of the room.

"Mother!" the old man croaked, his eyes open wide, staring at something that only he could see. "Mum's right there. She's waiting for me!"

The atmosphere in the room began to change. A veteran of numerous paranormal investigations, Amanda began to sense the presence of spirit activity within the room; it felt to her as if a great many people were coming together, gathering around the dying man's bed — a welcoming committee of sorts. She started to see flashes of light, sharp, bright, but distinct, dancing in front of her eyes.

She knew what that meant.

Giving her patient's hand a compassionate squeeze, she said, "Don't you worry, love. Your mum's here. She's come for you. She's going to take you home."

Her words of comfort caused the old man to smile nervously. Amanda continued to reassure him, waiting patiently by his side for him to take his last breath.

After a while, Amanda realized that she had to go and see to her other patients. Giving his hand one last reassuring squeeze, she got up and went about her business.

When she returned, the old man looked more peaceful than he had all day. She instinctively knew without checking that his pain was finally over. He was gone.

Suddenly, Amanda could see a bright white light appear in the area of the chair where her patient had seen his mother. A man and a woman stood there, outlined in glowing light. She recognized her patient, and from the way in which he smiled at the woman, was convinced that she could only have been his mother.

Slowly, the woman took the man's hand. Without looking back, the two spirits took a step forward, passing straight through the wall before disappearing.

After the official pronouncement of death had been

made, she felt the energy levels in the room slowly begin to dissipate. It wasn't long before everything had gone back to normal.

"Sometimes, when it comes to the very end of their life, people are afraid," Amanda says, looking back on the incident now. "It's only natural to be afraid…"

Stories of deceased loved ones coming to visit those who are dying are extremely common. Many palliative care providers have reported such occurrences.

While death is indeed a frightening thing to most people, the experience of having those who we have loved and lost return to help ease the transition seems to be a source of immense comfort.

Many people die peacefully, often with a smile on their face, as though relieved of the immense burden of physical living. This is particularly true when they have been suffering from a prolonged illness.

At the end of life, we seem to have nothing to fear except fear itself, as the old saying goes. As mortal beings, it is totally understandable for us to be frightened of losing our physical life and all that we have accrued during our lifetime. Yet countless mediums have agreed that we are only taking a step into a larger, better world, shedding our worn-out shell, which has about as much value and meaning once we have moved on as an old, threadbare piece of clothing that needs to be thrown away.

We may fear the process of dying, as it sometimes brings pain and discomfort, but so long as we have led a life worth living, we should never fear its ending.

CHAPTER TEN
A Sixth Sense?

One night, Amanda was working on the orthopedic ward at a large hospital in Melbourne. A young man in his twenties had been entrusted into her care. He had been involved in a high-speed car crash, and had sustained some very serious injuries. Although the doctors and nurses had him on the mend, he wasn't quite out of the woods just yet.

Something about the man seemed to be a little off, in Amanda's mind. She couldn't exactly put her finger on what it was, but she knew that *something* just wasn't quite right with her patient, and it was making her feel distinctly uneasy. She reported her concern to the sister in charge, who, rather than dismiss her instincts out of hand, agreed that Amanda should look in on him a little more frequently than normal that night.

Whether you want to call it instinct, intuition, the reading of subliminal cues and signals, or even some sort of sixth sense, many health care providers — especially nurses — are highly attuned to such things, and they tend to take them very seriously indeed — sometimes to the great benefit of their patients. Over the years of her nursing career,

Amanda has often heard one of her colleagues say, "It's going to be one of those shifts tonight," only for their prediction to be proven absolutely correct. Some of them also seem to be highly adept at predicting when a patient was going to die over the course of the next few hours.

This particular night was a quiet one on the ortho ward, which allowed Amanda the luxury of sitting and spending some extra time at the bedsides of some of her patients, usually the ones that were unable to sleep for one reason or another. Most often, the reason was because they missed their loved ones, or were homesick.

In accordance with her instincts, Amanda made a point of going to sit with the young car crash victim. He was still awake. They sat and talked for about an hour, mostly about trivial things.

Both of them suddenly began to notice flashes of light appearing and disappearing all around the room.

"What are those?" the young man asked, hardly able to believe his eyes. For Amanda, however, the light phenomena were nothing new. She explained that she and a number of other people believed such lights to be manifestations of the spirits of the dead. She went on to tell him that she had encountered them many times before in her life, and the two fell into deep conversation on the subject of the paranormal and life after death. The flashes continued to come and go as they talked, an ever-present light show in the background.

Lurking at the back of her mind while the two of them spoke was a nagging concern: Why had so many of these spirits gathered around this young man tonight? In her experience, they usually manifested when a person was close to death.

All of a sudden, Amanda was overcome with a wave of intense nausea, a feeling so strong that it was almost debilitating. She had been feeling perfectly calm and fine up until that point, but now she was filled with anxiety and a sense of great unease — there was no good reason for it that she could see, but by this stage of her nursing career, Amanda had learned to trust her feelings and impressions.

The young man began to convulse and jerk, his body going into a full-blown grand mal seizure. Amanda reacted instantly, calling out for the ward sister. She knew that the patient needed a benzodiazepine, a muscle relaxant such as diazepam, in order to break the seizure as soon as possible…otherwise his life was at risk.

The nursing team responded quickly and efficiently, working to stabilize the seizing young man. When his seizures were under control, they transferred him to the ICU. For her part, Amanda just went about her business for the remainder of her shift, tending to the rest of her patients, but her mind kept going back to the young man.

She was gravely concerned for his welfare. As things turned out, she had good reason to be.

On the following evening, Amanda was working on the same ward. She made a point of asking after him. The ward sister regarded her sadly and said, with great solemnity, "I'm sorry, but I'm afraid that he died. He threw a fat embolism."

Fat emboli are clumps of fat that can lodge in the blood vessels, obstructing the blood supply to the vital organs. They can be extremely difficult to diagnose, even by the very best medical professionals, and carry with them a high mortality rate.

Amanda was utterly crushed. It was as if she had been sucker-punched in the gut. Tears began streaming down her face.

"You'd better sit down," said the ward sister, helping her into a chair. Looking back on things with the benefit of hindsight, Amanda realizes that this was extremely unusual behavior for her. She was no stranger to patients dying, and was always very professional and composed in front of others; she might cry in private, particularly if she had developed an emotional bond with the patient in question, but she was not given to breaking down like that.

Despite the fact that she had never met the young man before yesterday, and had spent little more than an hour in his company, she was reacting as if she had been told that a loved one had died.

The ward nurse went to fetch her a glass of water. As she sat in the chair, trying to compose herself, Amanda suddenly felt what she could only describe as a vortex of cold air swirling all around her. She went from being hot and flushed to cool and chilled in the space of a few seconds. Then came a strong gust of cold air, directly in her face, almost as though it was being directed there by somebody she couldn't see.

Could it be that the spirit of the young man had come back to visit her, and that this was his way of affirming that he had survived the death of his physical body?

Although somewhat reassured, Amanda felt drained and out-of-sorts for the rest of the night. Nevertheless, she drank the glass of water, got to her feet, and went to take care of her patients.

Get knocked down. Pick yourself up. Dust yourself off.

Get on with the job.

    No matter what, that's just what nurses do.

One of the golden rules of paranormal investigation is this: one should never arrive at a paranormal explanation before thoroughly considering and ruling out the multitude of mundane, everyday alternatives.

    As the great Sir Arthur Conan Doyle said, "Once we have eliminated the possible, whatever remains, however improbable, must be the truth."

    In the case of the nursing instinct or 'sixth sense,' which allows some of them to apparently predict when a patient is going to die during their watch, it should be borne in mind that we are talking about highly-educated, skilled, and experienced clinicians. It is entirely possible that the "hunch" concerning the patient's death is actually the result of them having subconsciously processed a considerable number of factors and scraps of information during their assessment of the patient and the situation. These factors could include (but are not necessarily limited to) the blood pressure, heart rate, respiratory rate, laboratory values, electrocardiogram, mental status, skin signs, and a hundred other clinical variables, not least including the very basic but all-important question: "Does the patient *look* sick?"

A good nurse, doctor, or field medic will incorporate all of these findings into building up a mental picture of the patient's overall medical status, and they will quite frequently do so without even thinking about it consciously, in the same way that you probably do not think consciously about speeding up, slowing down, changing lanes, and the behavior of other vehicles on the road while driving, because you have done it so many times and have therefore learned to calculate it all while running on autopilot.

In short, this instinct is most likely not paranormal at all, in my view, at least; rather, I suspect that it is a measure of the skill and experience level attained by the care provider over the course of their medical career. The longer they serve, the more sharply-honed – and therefore more accurate – this instinct becomes.

CHAPTER ELEVEN
The Departing Soul

Those who believe in the existence of a spirit, soul, or whatever you choose to call the energy life force that comprises and animates us all, often wonder whether there are any physical manifestations taking place when the body dies and that energy is ultimately released.

The literature of paranormal research is replete with a diverse range of accounts and observations of this process taking place. Perhaps the most widely-known attempt to scientifically test the validity of the soul having some form of material existence was the now-infamous '21 Grams Experiment,' conducted in 1901 by Dr. Duncan MacDougall.

MacDougall's concept was a simple one: if the human spirit or soul had any form of mass whatsoever, then he *should* — theoretically speaking, and given a sufficiently sensitive weighing apparatus — be able to detect a change in mass, once the soul had departed the physical body and headed off for pastures new.

He made arrangements to weigh the bodies of six terminally-ill patients. As the point of death approached,

MacDougall placed their bodies on a scale which was so accurate that, when properly calibrated, was capable of detecting even the tiniest changes in weight. For good measure, he also weighed the bodies of several dogs as they died. MacDougall was nothing if not a completist.

To this day, the results of this experiment remain controversial — although most scientists and physicians agree that a sample size of six patients is far too small a statistical base from which to derive meaningful results. Although some of the patients did indeed lose a very small amount of weight after death (with the greatest amount being 21.3 grams, hence the retroactive naming of the experiment) skeptics have rightly pointed out that peri- and post-mortem fluid loss through the pores of the skin in the form of sweat could potentially explain that. Supporting the skeptical case even further is the fact that none of the canines lost any weight, and dogs do not sweat at all.

At the time of writing, some 117 years later, nobody has seen fit to repeat MacDougall's experiment, despite the advances in technology and medicine that the 21st century has brought.

Although science has yet to prove or disprove the existence of a soul, there is no shortage of eyewitness accounts from the bedsides of dying patients which suggest that *something* often appears to leave the human body at the moment of death.

Amanda was caring for an elderly gentleman one evening when she experienced one of the strangest events of her entire life. Her patient was dying of cancer, and sadly had no friends or family members to support him during his final days. For this reason, Amanda made it a priority to spend as much time as she possibly could in keeping him company. After all, she believed that nobody should ever have to die all alone.

After she had made her evening rounds of the ward, Amanda went to the old man's bedside and sat with him, just holding his hand and reassuring him quietly. He had already slipped into a state of unconsciousness, and before long, she began to recognize the tell-tale signs of death drawing near. His breathing came in longer, slower gasps, until finally deteriorating into the harsh rasps of what medical professionals refer to as agonal breathing — what is more commonly known as the 'death rattle.'

This patient had the equivalent of the DNR, which in Australia is known as an NFR (Not For Resuscitation) order, so there was little for Amanda to do except continue to keep him company and talk softly. At one point, she offered up a short prayer.

"It's okay for you to go," she whispered in his ear. "You don't have to stay here. There is no need for you to be afraid. If you can see a light, it is alright for you to go toward it."

The lights above the patient's bed began to flicker off and on. Amanda had witnessed this before at the bedside of a patient who was actively dying. This was more than a simple power brown-out: the lights flared brilliantly, flashing and dimming over and over again.

What happened next was something that she had definitely *not* seen before. The side-rail of the bed began to judder violently, as though somebody had grasped it and was shaking it for all that they were worth. The patient himself wasn't convulsing. Amanda was still holding his hand, and confirmed that the man's body itself was totally still. Only the *side* of the bed was affected, though by what, exactly, she could not say.

Suddenly, a dark column of smoke came swirling up out of the man's chest. It shot straight up and disappeared through the ceiling titles above them both.

Just as quickly as it had begun, the experience was over. Amanda checked her patient's body over carefully, confirming that he was no longer breathing and that his heart had stopped beating.

The lights in the room flared once more and then returned to normal, leaving the nurse to sit silently for a moment, lost in her own thoughts.

Had she just witnessed the actual moment of a human soul leaving the body? If so, what an immense privilege and blessing had been bestowed upon her.

CHAPTER TWELVE
Fatal Mistakes

Over the course of his life, Rick has worked in hospitals and nursing homes for more than forty years, primarily as an orderly, cleaner, and theater technician. At the time of writing, Rick works as a hospital orderly in Australia.

In his own time, he is a psychic medium for the Australian Paranormal Society (APS), satisfying a curiosity for all things spiritual and paranormal that has existed since he was a teenager.

"All around the world, somebody passes away in a hospital or nursing home every second," Rick points out, "which explains why they are such active places. When you work in one, you do get to know some of the people who pass, usually of old age or a terminal illness."

As part of his job, Rick quite often finds himself removing the bodies of the newly-deceased, and transporting them down to the morgue, waiting with the body until the funeral director's staff comes to collect it.

"When you do this kind of work often, you not only develop a respect for the living, but also for their spirits," he explains. "I always make a point of teaching those who are interested in understanding the nature of spirit that spirits are people too…They were once in their own physical body, undergoing their own journey through life."

By the time he first started working in the hospital setting, Rick's mother had died. Several unusual encounters relating to her death only served to cement his belief in the paranormal even further, and yet losing her had also raised a host of questions concerning the subject of what lies between life and death.

Although he had seen spirit energies as a youth, Rick says that true understanding only came when he began to work in the healthcare field — more specifically, as a cleaner at a geriatric hospital.

Rick was asked to go into one of the patient rooms and buff the floor with a polishing machine. The room was built to accommodate four people, but three of the beds were empty. The fourth bed was surrounded by a drawn curtain. Although he was initially concerned about disturbing the sleeping resident, Rick was assured that it would be fine for him to go in and start polishing.

Wanting to do a thorough job, Rick spent a good eight to ten minutes working on the floor, getting into every nook and cranny with the machine. Nothing stirred behind the closed curtains, and he couldn't quite shake the feeling that he really ought to take a look and see what it was that they concealed.

Rick switched the polishing machine off and walked across the room, being careful not to smear the gleaming, newly-shined floor. Slowly, as quietly as he could manage, Rick drew the curtain aside.

An elderly lady lay in the bed, her eyes closed, sleeping peacefully…Yet on closer inspection, Rick realized that her chest didn't seem to be rising and falling at all. For a few moments he simply stood there, watching her, compelled to do so by a feeling that was difficult to put into words.

Leaning in a little closer, he discovered that she was in fact still breathing, although each breath was faint and shallow.

Suddenly, a slight haze began to rise up from the old woman's body. Rick rubbed at his eyes, thinking that he might be seeing things. But there it was, a plain as day; the mist rose upward, like a lighter version of the plume of smoke above a campfire. As it neared the ceiling, the haze gradually seemed to dissipate, finally disappearing into thin air.

After thinking about it for a while, Rick ultimately

concluded that he must have just borne witness to the old lady's soul leaving her body for the last time.

Leaving the room, Rick ran into the nurse who was responsible for the patients on this particular stretch of the ward. "You might want to go in and check on the lady in that room," he told her, pointing toward the curtained-off bed. "I think she just passed on."

"I very much doubt it," the nurse said, raising one eyebrow. "I'm pretty sure she's got a few more days left in her yet."

"Would you humor me and look in on her anyway?"

The nurse said that she would. Mollified, Rick went about his business. A few hours later, he ran into the nurse a second time.

"How did you know that the old lady had passed?" she asked him, without preamble. Fully expecting her to think that he was a little strange, Rick nevertheless recounted what he had seen, going into great detail about the unusual mist he had watched rise up from the elderly lady's body. Instead, the nurse's face lit up in delight.

"I've seen that too!" she exclaimed, full of excitement. "The exact same mist. I'm so glad I'm not the only one — I thought I was imagining it!"

Rick happened to be working late one night when his pager went off unexpectedly. Puzzled, he unclipped it from his belt and checked the phone number. It was one of the cleaning ladies who also worked overnight shifts. She and a couple of her colleagues were all assigned to clean up one of the operating theaters upstairs. Apparently, she wanted to talk to him.

"Hey, it's me, Rick," he said, after picking up a nearby phone and dialing her number. "What's up?"

He could tell straight away that there was something a little off from the tone of her voice. "Do you think you could come up here to the theater, Rick?" she asked, sounding ever so slightly embarrassed.

Rick realized that something strange must have happened up there. It wasn't as if the three of them needed help cleaning the place, and Rick was well-known around the hospital for being 'one of those ghost guys.'

"I'll be right there."

Hanging up the phone, Rick took an elevator a few floors up to the operating theater, where he found the cleaner to be a little on edge. She went on to explain that she had been minding her own business, thoroughly cleaning the floors and surfaces in the operating theater, when all of a sudden, she had heard the sound of a very loud expletive, apparently coming right out of thin air. It had been a man's voice, coarse and angry, and all the more frightening given the fact that there were no men present in the room at the time.

The worst was yet to come. Still upset from hearing the disembodied voice, she was looking around the theater, trying to figure out who possibly could have spoken, when an invisible fist slammed her full-force in the stomach. The cleaner doubled over, groaning in pain. Rick looked down at her hands. No wonder they were still shaking.

"Let me have a look around," he said, giving her a reassuring pat on the shoulder. Walking slowly around the room, Rick searched high and low for the source of the voice, methodically checking each and every shadow. He reached the far wall, still empty-handed…and then came the growl.

It was low and threatening. Just as the cleaner had described, it seemed to originate from — nowhere.

"F*** OFF!"

It was a male voice, almost certainly the same one that the cleaner had heard, and it sounded less than pleased with Rick. He looked around, once again confirming that there wasn't a man lurking somewhere inside the theater. Needless to say, there wasn't.

Under those same circumstances, most people would have been quaking in their boots. But Rick wasn't most people. Not only was he an Aussie bloke, born and bred, but he was also extremely familiar with the behavior of spirit entities. This one was trying to scare him, for reasons best known only to itself, and he was having none of it.

Instead of running from the theater screaming, Rick casually told the spirit, "You can go and f*** off yourself, mate."

The entity was apparently chastened when Rick stood up to it, because it never pushed back. At least, Rick didn't find himself getting punched in the guts, and the voice didn't pipe up and speak to him again.

He waited around for a while, but no more paranormal activity took place that he could detect. A little nervously, the cleaners went back about their business, only too glad when their work in that particular theater was over and done with for the night.

It wasn't long, however, before the entity was back at its old tricks. Reports began to reach Rick of objects being thrown violently around in the same theater, clattering noisily and causing plenty of distraction. Strange sounds were heard. Worst of all, a few days after they had first paged him asking for help, a member of the night shift cleaning crew was smacked in the head by another invisible force.

So far as Rick was concerned, that was the final straw. Paranormal activity was one thing, but he wouldn't stand for violence.

He was going to get to the bottom of this once and for all.

Heading up to the darkened operating theater late one night, he set his cell phone camera to video mode and started it recording, placing it carefully on one of the flat surfaces. Then he left it alone to do its thing.

He could sense a form of spirit energy in there, a cold, angry presence that seemed to take great delight in inducing fear whenever the opportunity arose for it to do so.

An hour or so later, he went back to collect his phone. Sitting down to review the footage, Rick's suspicions were confirmed: the video camera had captured the presence of a tall, shadowy figure, walking along the gloomy corridor right at the very edge of the frame.

The next step was obvious. Rick had mediumistic

abilities, after all. Whoever or whatever it was, he was going to go up there and attempt to make contact with it.

Deliberately leaving the lights out, he sat down in the center of the pitch-black theater and spoke openly, inviting the spirit to come and talk to him.

He didn't have long to wait.

The spirit surged forward angrily, yelling and screaming obscenities at him. Rick kept his cool, calmly asking the entity why it was so angry and just what exactly did it want?

"What's your problem?"

After a few more heated insults and curses were hurled at him, Rick finally sensed that the spirit energy was beginning to calm down a little. He wasn't fighting anger with more anger — the psychic equivalent of pouring gasoline on a barbecue — but rather, he was refusing to engage it in confrontation, thereby preventing an already tense situation from escalating even further.

It turned out to be exactly the right approach.

With just a little coaxing, the spirit ultimately revealed the source of its great anger. It — or rather, *he* — was furious at the doctor who had, in his eyes at least, allowed him to die on the operating table in that theater.

"He made a damn mistake!" the spirit raged. "And it cost

me my *life!*"

Seeing it from the spirit's perspective caused Rick to have a great deal of sympathy. That was a totally understandable cause for any soul to harbor such great resentment.

"I can see why you're so angry," he told the man's spirit, "but the cleaners didn't play any part in what happened to you…so just lay off them, okay?"

The two men, one flesh and blood, one in a spirit body, stayed and chatted with one another for a while. A bond of trust was ultimately established between them, so much so in fact that the man even gave Rick his name. Rick was able to go and check the hospital records and confirm that a male patient had indeed died on the operating table in that very same theater. His death was due to one of the many 'complications' that are a regrettable but usually unavoidable occurrence in the field of surgery.

When they finally parted ways, Rick left with a solemn promise that the spirit would no longer abuse the cleaning staff or any of the medical professionals that performed surgery in the operating theater.

True to his word, the entity did indeed stop bothering the living, and for the night shift cleaners, the operating room went from being a place of fear to just another stop along their work route.

As for the ghost of the man who had died on the table, well…Rick left the hospital soon after to take another job. For all he knows, the spirit may still be keeping a silent watch over every surgery that takes place there, making sure that there are no more fatal mistakes…

CHAPTER THIRTEEN
The Man in the Body Bag

The hospital was old, which was rather fitting in light of the fact that its primary focus was to care for the elderly. A group of interconnected buildings were linked by a series of covered walkways.

It was late at night when Rick happened to be traveling along one of those walkways, heading from one ward to the next. He was still fairly new there, but liked the job and his co-workers a great deal, and found that he was fitting right in.

Rick looked down at his watch and saw that it was already half-past midnight. He quickened his pace. There was still a lot to be done before the night shift was over.

Up ahead, he was surprised to see the figure of a young girl skipping along the walkway, passing from one pool of shadow to another. From what he could see from twenty meters away, she appeared to be no more than six or seven years old, at most.

That's strange, Rick thought to himself, *what's a young girl doing, roaming around a hospital at this time of the morning?*

Perhaps she was the grandchild of one of the patients, he mused, though it seemed awfully late for her to still be awake, let alone unattended by her parents. Besides, visiting hours had finished long ago. The hospital was supposed to have been secured until the morning.

"Hello, there!" Rick called out. "Are you alright? Are you lost?"

If she heard him at all, the young girl chose to ignore him. She simply continued to skip her way along the hallway, apparently lost in her own private world.

More than a little perturbed, Rick decided to follow the girl. He quickened his pace, but still didn't seem to catch up with her. She skipped straight past the patient ward that had been Rick's original destination, and instead made her way to an administrative building that housed mostly office space and equipment storage.

Turning to skip along a side corridor, the young girl went down a flight of stairs and into another hallway, one that led outside to a grassy field which the hospital staff referred to as 'the Oval.' The hallway had no doors along either side of it, and was completely devoid of places to hide.

Rick reached the bottom of the staircase and looked around. He was puzzled. The little girl was nowhere to be seen. She couldn't possibly have reached the single set of doors that led outside, which both stood closed. Where had she gone?

He searched the area just to be sure, even going so far as to poke his head outside. The Oval was dark, silent, and completely devoid of life.

Heading back to the ward that had been his original destination, Rick asked the on-duty nurses if they had seen a little girl skipping around the hospital that night. None of them had. Had there perhaps been a family visiting one of their patients? The answer was once again no; sadly, there had been no visitors at all that evening.

Although he knew that he really ought to let the matter drop, Rick's curiosity now got the better of him. He continued to ask about the mysterious little girl that he had seen. Finally, after speaking to one of the longest-serving nurses in the entire hospital, he found his answer.

Back in the 1930s, the hospital had been a specialist facility for children afflicted with polio. The nurse told him that many times over the decades, the apparition of a young girl had been seen, skipping along the very same hallway where Rick had encountered her. She would never respond when spoken to, the nurse explained, but simply continued on her merry way, seemingly without a care in the world, before disappearing from sight at the bottom of the staircase that led out to the Oval — the ghost of a child long since dead, repeating a journey she had first made more than seventy years before…and skipping her way into eternity.

It is a universally-accepted truth among members of the medical profession that no matter the skill level of the doctors, nurses, and technicians, patients are still going to die sooner or later. This means that most hospitals have a morgue of some sort (although some smaller facilities may send the bodies of the newly-deceased directly to the coroner's office or mortician).

Some morgues are larger than others, of course. In smaller hospitals, the space set aside for temporarily housing the dead is nothing more than a single room, capable of holding only three or four bodies at a time. In bigger, busier metropolitan hospitals, particularly those that serve as major trauma centers, the capacity for storing refrigerated corpses is much greater, in order to meet the increased demand.

I have spoken to a number of undertakers and morticians over the years who have told me — usually off the record, for fear of being ridiculed or adversely affecting their business — of paranormal occurrences that have happened to them in funeral parlors and mortuaries. Small wonder, then, that a number of hospital morgues should have their share of ghost stories too.

Forensic pathologist Putri Dianita recounted her own ghostly experience on the following quora.com thread:
https://www.quora.com/What-is-it-like-in-the-morgue-at-a-hospital

> *One such event was when I came in one early morning not long after I started working there. I was just passing through the entrance hall leading to the offices. I saw one of my supervisors having a chat with one of my colleagues. Another colleague, let's call her "Ani", was just sitting quietly listening to the other two talk. "Ani" was wearing our usual blue scrubs that we usually wear while on duty. After saying Hi, I went down the corridor and upstairs to the office. When I opened the office door, lo and behold, "Ani" was sitting in front of her computer typing a report! And she was wearing a pink blouse! There was no way she could have run ahead of me to the office because the corridor is a narrow one, neither are there any other staircases. I was pretty*

dumbfounded, but I thought that those kind of things simply go with the job…

Generally speaking, morgues are located in the hospital basement, discreetly tucked away from the prying eyes of the general public, most of whom do not like to be reminded of the presence of death (and therefore their own mortality) in any way, shape, or form.

The hospital in which Rick now works is no exception. The on-site morgue is hidden away behind an anonymous-looking door below ground. It sees more than its fair share of paranormal activity, particularly at night, when the shadows seem to take on a life of their own. Doors open on their own and then slam themselves shut again, despite the fact that there are no natural or artificial breezes or drafts that could make them move.

Rick and the night supervisor have both witnessed these phenomena on multiple occasions, and have grown so used to it that it no longer fazes them. They tend to write such strange occurrences off with a shrug, figuring that somebody just isn't ready to go yet…

Nor is the morgue the only part of the hospital where the shadows move. Nursing staff have often seen elevator doors open by themselves, with nobody inside the car to operate it. Dark figures walk in and out of empty patient rooms late at night, and the nurses know better than to pry into their business. They leave the shadow figures alone, and in return, hope that these mysterious nocturnal visitors will do the same for them.

The hospital ghost sightings take place fairly consistently all year round, but each year without fail, the hazy apparitions of several phantom nuns are often seen, always at about the same time and in the same general area: close to the second level. Rick has encountered them himself, and can attest to the accuracy of the sightings.

Perhaps the strangest encounter with the ghostly nuns happened when a group of nurses were looking out of the second-floor windows that overlook the parking structure late one night. Out there in the darkness, they were astonished to see the figures of several shadowy nuns gliding along through thin air, floating as though standing on a floor that has long since disappeared.

At the time of writing (2018) the hospital that Rick works at is only ten years old. A good paranormal investigator knows that it is not the age of the building that matters, but rather the events that took place on that same stretch of ground over the preceding decades and centuries. Countless lives may have been lived on that same ground, each one full of love, hope, despair, anger, joy, and the countless emotions that fill up every human life to the brim. Where there is life there is also drama, and where one finds strong emotion and dramatic activity, one often also finds ghosts.

The current hospital sits on the site of a much older hospital, one which was demolished to make way for its newer successor. A significant part of the old structure was located where the parking garage now stands. As it was built in the 1800s by the Catholic church, it made sense that the spirits of long-dead nuns should haunt it to this day — still going about their holy duties years after leaving their physical bodies behind...

Also to be found on the hospital grounds is an old manor house, which was built back in the 1860s. It is used primarily for administrative purposes these days, and as such is only open during office hours.

The technicians whose job it is to carry out maintenance on the manor house are not exactly fond of the place, not least because the fire alarms have developed the curious habit of going off for no apparent reason, most often late at night. This happens several times a month, and every time the alarms go off, the fire brigade has no choice but to respond. This has cost the hospital a small fortune in false alarm fines, yet no matter how many times the experts go over the alarm system, they can find nothing wrong with it.

Something is obviously tripping the sensors…the question is, what is the nature of that something? Could it perhaps have something to do with the topmost floor, which has a reputation for being haunted by the tragic ghosts of the former lady of the house, whose tenure dates back to its days as a private residence? After the death of her children, the grief-stricken lady is said to have climbed the bell tower and taken her own life by hanging herself.

It may be that her spirit is the one responsible for setting off the fire alarm. Or perhaps it is one of her lost children, running and playing in the rooms and hallways that were their playground in life, blissfully oblivious to the fact that they are actually long since dead…

One day, Rick and his partner were called upon to help transport the body of a newly-deceased patient from the room in which they had died, down to the hospital mortuary.

The two men dutifully approached the patent's room, bringing a wheeled trolley along with them. Stepping through the open doorway, Rick immediately caught sight of a featureless black body bag stretched out on the bed. From how bulked out it was, he could tell that the bag was most definitely occupied. Obviously, other members of the hospital staff had gotten there before him and had zipped the deceased's body up prior to it being moved. That wasn't an uncommon thing to have happen. The nurses and orderlies were an efficient bunch, and didn't like to leave their dead patients' remains laying around for too long. After all, bed space was at a premium, and there was no shortage of living patients to claim what the dead no longer needed.

Rick went into the room, being careful not to hit anything with the trolley. Looking up, he couldn't help but notice the figure of a man at the far end of the bed, the same end at which the deceased patient's feet could be found. He was pacing up and down along the side of the bed, his head held in his hands, obviously deeply upset by something or other.

"Why am I in a bag?" he moaned, clearly in significant distress. "Why have they covered me up? *What are they doing to me?!?!*"

Even before the man had spoken, Rick had guessed that this must be the spirit of the patient who had occupied this room. His form was slightly transparent, just like the stereotypical phantoms that we have all seen on TV and in the movies.

Asking his very non-psychic partner to please step out of the room in order to fetch some stickers for the record book, Rick gently closed the door behind him so that he and the anxious spirit could have a little privacy.

"Hang on a minute!" the dead man exclaimed, looking Rick straight in the eye. "You can *see* me?"

Nodding, Rick confirmed that he could indeed see him. Instead of calming him down, this surprising bit of information only seemed to panic the spirit even more.

"Why did they cover me up like that?" he sobbed. "I don't understand what's going on!"

Deep down, of course, the man really *did* know. Standing over his own lifeless body, watching in horror as the hospital staff placed it into a body bag and sealed it up, meant that there was really only one conclusion to be reached. But denial is a very powerful thing, and this poor soul simply wasn't ready or willing to accept the truth that he had drawn his final breath just yet.

Fortunately, this was where being a psychic medium can come in very handy. Taking a deep breath, Rick began to explain to the man that yes, he was, in fact, dead. As the spirit burst out into even more sobs, he held his hands out to try and calm him down a bit.

"You know that's your body right there in front of you," Rick went on, gesturing at the bag that still lay motionless on the bed in front of them. "There's no going back to it, no matter how much you might want to. It's like a set of worn-out old clothes that are no longer fit to wear. They can't be mended. But don't worry, mate…The good news is, you can go off now and get yourself a brand-new set!"

That stopped the dead man in his tracks. He asked Rick exactly what he meant by that.

"That old thing was never you," Rick said, still indicating the body bag. "You were — and you *are* — so much more than just a physical body. All of your friends, family, and loved ones are waiting for you over there on the other side, mate. All you have to do is look up, look towards the light, and find the strength to go toward it."

"I don't know," the spirit said doubtfully. "What's it like over there?"

"A whole lot better than it is over here on this side! That's our *true* home, the place where we all come from, and the place where we must all go back to someday. And today's *your* day. It's a cause for celebration, not for tears."

As he talked out loud to the spirit of the newly-deceased patient, Rick was mentally calling out to ask any member of the dead man's family to come and assist in helping him cross over to the next world.

True to Rick's word, when the man looked up toward the corner of the room, he saw that a bright light had appeared above him. A figure began to emerge from it, somebody that the spirit obviously recognized, because it brought a broad smile to his face. Rick could tell that the newcomer was a female, though specific details were difficult to make out. The dead man's facial expression was now one of absolute relief. As the woman held out a hand, he reached out to accept it, and allowed her to lead him backward into the blinding light from which she had just emerged.

Finally, when both of the spirits had faded into it, the light suddenly dimmed and vanished, leaving Rick all alone in the hospital room with the last physical remnants of the departed man.

Although he has been fortunate enough to witness people leaving this realm on more than one occasion, the experience, which Rick says is "absolutely indescribable,' rarely fails to move him to tears…tears of joy.

Those tears came on this occasion too, as he simply stood there, he eyes moistening and his heart full of gladness, contemplating the joyous family reunion that was just kicking off on the other side of the veil.

CHAPTER FOURTEEN
The Lady in White

Sometimes, especially when they both do the same job, it is possible for two people to meet for the very first time only to discover that they instantly get on like a house on fire.

Such was the case when I met Luis. It's a night that I will never forget, simply because of the place where we met: now one of my favorite haunted locations, Iowa's notorious Malvern Manor. Once a hotel, then a residential nursing facility, this ramshackle old building has seen more than its fair share of human drama over the decades, and as a result its long-abandoned rooms and hallways are blessed with an abundance of ghosts.

Luis knows pretty much everything there is to know about the history and the haunting of this grand old place. He has spent countless hours not only investigating its many secrets, but also giving ghost tours to sightseers that come from near and far in order to sample the atmosphere for themselves.

I moved into Malvern Manor for a few days with a team of like-minded paranormal investigators (for those who may be interested, my book about the Malvern haunting and our research into it is called *The Devil's Coming to Get Me: The Haunting of Malvern Manor*). Luis and I hit it off immediately, not least because we were both paramedics, and therefore talked a common language.

When he learned that I was writing this book, Luis offered up a work-related ghost story of his own. A co-founder and field investigator for the Omne Paranormal Society, Luis was also well-versed in the arena of paranormal investigation.

His story took place in a hospital where he once worked in the lab. Knowing of his interest in all things ghostly, the nurses were delighted to tell him about the building's resident spirit.

The hospital was said to be haunted by the ghost of a nurse from times long past, they said. The apparition was always described as wearing a nursing uniform, the early twentieth century white affair complete with white shoes, stockings, and a hat.

The phantom nurse was most commonly encountered in the oldest part of the hospital, which had long since been converted into classrooms and an administrative area. She would walk from room to room, in the manner of any nurse making her rounds and checking in on all of her patients.

Luis was working an overnight shift when he had his own encounter with the phantom nurse. It just so happened that the break room assigned to the laboratory technicians was located in that particular part of the building, with its doorway opening out onto a central corridor. After finishing his assigned break, Luis had just emerged into that same hallway when he caught a glimpse of a woman walking away from him at the opposite end.

At first glance, he thought that she was a patient or a late-night visitor that had lost their way. Concerned that she might be in need of some assistance, Luis headed after her, his shoes squeaking on the tile floor the only sound that could be heard.

Reaching the end of the hallway, he was puzzled to find that the lady was nowhere to be seen.

That's a little odd, he thought to himself, but shrugged it off and went back to work. His brain hadn't put two and two together yet. The lady had been about five feet five inches tall, he estimated, and wearing a plain white dress, which was very different to the scrubs that his modern-day colleagues wore. He had also not realized that the hat she was wearing was an old-fashioned nursing hat, as he only caught sight of it from the back, and even then it was just for an instant.

Luis checked all of the surrounding corridors and the rooms that branched off from them. There was nobody to be found. Yet there was no way the woman could have gotten past him.

Returning to his lab, Luis took a seat at his desk and began to run the blood tests that were the bread and butter of his job. But the strange encounter nagged at him. After a few minutes, he went out to check the hallways again.

Nothing.

He returned to work, but his mind just wouldn't focus on it. Luis realized that he was beginning to fixate on the sighting of the mysterious woman. With a frustrated sigh, he got to his feet and went back out into the corridor a third time…

…and there she was.

This time, the lady in white was walking towards him, and although she was still at the far end of the hallway, she gave Luis a good view of her face and form. That's when the penny finally dropped, and he recognized the old-fashioned nursing uniform for what it truly was.

When he checked with the duty nurses the following day, several of them admitted to having seen the ghostly nurse themselves during their time at the hospital, and all of their descriptions matched the woman that Luis had seen down to the very last detail. There could be no reasonable doubt that they had all encountered the same figure, an echo from years gone by, still discharging her sacred duty to the nursing vocation long after her physical death.

Some of those same nurses also reported the doors opening and closing all by themselves on the educational wing (the doors would once have been those to individual patient rooms) and to have heard the sound of voices calling out incomprehensible words from rooms that hadn't hosted a living patient in decades.

The phantom nurse's behavior was always the same: walking slowly along the hallways, methodically moving from room to room — none of which had contained an actual patient for decades — going about her ghostly rounds.

Intrigued by what he now knew to be a ghost sighting, Luis was very much in favor of investigating further, digging into the history of the location and going through some of the archive photographs of the nurses who worked there many years ago. Unfortunately, the powers that be at the hospital tended to frown upon any mention of their resident spirit, preferring to downplay the numerous sightings as being nothing more than ghost stories. Conducting anything even resembling true paranormal research would be out of the question.

The real identity of the phantom nurse therefore remains, for the foreseeable future at least, a mystery.

Stories of doctors and nurses staying 'on the job' long after they have passed away are surprisingly common in the annals of paranormal research. One can only admire the compassion and sense of duty that must be required in order to carry on working from beyond the grave…

CHAPTER FIFTEEN
Escaping our Demons

As a tour guide at Iowa's notoriously haunted Edinburgh Manor, Becky is no stranger to all things ghostly. In her everyday life, she is a social worker who carries out home health visits for Medicaid patients, which puts her firmly among the ranks of medical professionals.

As part of her assigned duties, she spends a great deal of time visiting people in nursing homes. It is a difficult and usually an unsung, under-appreciated field of endeavor.

Becky has had a lifelong interest in the paranormal, but says that for many years she "kept her wall up," essentially shutting herself off from those kinds of phenomena. Her own healthcare-related paranormal experiences mostly took place in her old stomping ground of the Ozarks, back when she was working in a behavioral health clinic.

The clinic was housed in an old nursing home. Most of the workers' offices were located along one particular hallway. The hallway had something of a reputation for being haunted, and the employees would tell stories about the spirits they believed could be found there.

Becky's own office was not on the so-called 'haunted

hallway,' which she found to be a bit of a disappointment. Being the paranormal enthusiast that she was, she made every excuse imaginable to go and visit her co-workers down there, hanging out as much as possible and hoping for a ghostly encounter of her own.

Two neighboring offices were known for experiencing a rather strange phenomenon. A phone extension in one of the rooms would regularly call its neighbor in the room next door, even when neither of the offices were occupied.

Telephone engineers looked at the problem from every technical angle imaginable, but all attempts to troubleshoot the issue came to naught. It was as if an invisible somebody really wanted to speak to another invisible somebody sitting just a few feet away, and would keep on calling until they finally got what they wanted.

The phantom phone calls became so frequent that they soon grew into a genuine annoyance, eating into office productivity time. When one of the workers was sitting at her desk, the phone would ring. She would of course pick it up, and more often than not, nobody was at the other end.

The silent call *always* originated in the office next door.

Becky saw this happen personally on numerous occasions.

One day, Becky was leaning in the doorway of one of the haunted offices, hanging out with a colleague and pretty much minding her own business, when she heard footsteps coming up behind her in the hallway. The plodding steps got louder and louder, finally stopping just a short distance behind her. Becky heard what sounded like a man's sigh, and felt his breath on the back of her neck.

Turning around to laugh at her co-worker for his creepy scare tactics, she was dumbfounded to find that the hallway was completely empty. The sigh, the sensation of breath on her skin, had all been one hundred percent real. She knew beyond all shadow of a doubt that she had not imagined them.

Rather than finding the experience frightening, however, Becky remembers it as being "pretty cool."

Not every situation she encountered while working there could be described in that way...

Becky will never forget one particular home health visit for as long as she lives. The patient in question, a gentleman in his fifties, had been diagnosed with schizophrenia some thirty years before. While a deeply misunderstood and stigmatized condition, schizophrenia can nonetheless induce terrifyingly violent behavior in those who are afflicted with it.

She had developed a close rapport with her patient, as all good care givers do whenever possible, and the man had opened up to her, telling Becky that ever since his very first boyhood memories, he could recall seeing shadowy figures flitting around his bedroom. The shadow figures would often wake him up at night, standing over his bed. As he grew older and became a teenager, he finally summoned up the courage to tell his parents what was happening. Their immediate response was to send him to a psychiatrist for a mental health evaluation.

One afternoon, Becky was sitting with the patient in his living room, making small talk and asking him how things were going. As the conversation entered more serious territory, with Becky assessing the severity of his depression and emotional state as best she could, she started to notice that her patient was becoming distracted. Although he seemed to be earnestly trying to focus on her and what she was saying, something else kept catching the man's eye.

Gently, she asked him whether his 'visions' (as he preferred to call them) were still happening. The man fell silent.

"You're seeing something now, aren't you?" Becky coaxed him, her voice gentle.

"Yeah," he admitted.

"What are you seeing?"

Although obviously reluctant, her patient described what he called "three or four demons" standing behind her in the far corner of the room. The presence of these dark figures had plagued him for years.

"They're always here," the man stated flatly, his voice an unsettling monotone. "Always in the living room…"

With hindsight, Becky wonders just how much of what this poor fellow experienced could be laid at the door of his mental illness, and how much of it may have been something entirely different…something far more alarming.

Her patient had been tormented by the presence of shadow figures for almost his entire life. The vast array of medications that his doctors had prescribed in a vain attempt to help him had had little to no effect, and while Becky watched him as he in turn looked back and forth between her and the invisible figures, she could tell that he was growing increasingly agitated.

"How many people are wrongly diagnosed with a

behavioral disorder, when the source of their problem is actually paranormal?" she asked during our interview. "And on the flip side, how many cases in which somebody thinks they are being haunted are really caused by mental illness?"

It is a point well-made. Throughout the course of recorded history, unfortunate individuals were declared to be possessed by demons and evil spirits, undergoing a rite of exorcism (or something similar) in order to free them…only to die choking in their own spittle because what they were *truly* suffering from was a grand mal seizure, the medical term for full-body convulsions, which are often fatal if the proper medications are not administered in a timely manner.

The discipline of behavioral health itself is in its infancy when compared to the broader field of medicine. Consider the fact that doctors only stopped performing ice pick lobotomies — the barbaric practice of inserting a sharpened ice pick into the eye socket and hammering it home until its tip made contact with the frontal lobe of the brain — some sixty years ago. Despite the many advances that physicians have made in this area, the raw truth is that many medications and alternative therapies are relatively ineffective in the face of some of the more serious diseases.

Better therapies are being worked on, and studies are

being continuously undertaken, but our understanding of mental illness and the best ways to treat it is advancing at a very slow rate.

Becky's patient began to tell her about the figure that he was seeing, describing it as being black in color and somewhere around nine feet tall. It was extremely thin, solid, and though it had a human-shaped head, the figure had only a pair of recessed yellow eyes, sunken into a featureless black miasma where its face ought to have been.

The other shadow figures were almost identical in appearance, he claimed, but none of them were quite as tall as the one which appeared to be the leader of the pack.

"Okay, I see you," the man said, talking to the shadow figure. He explained that usually, when he acknowledged the presence of the black figures out loud, they would disappear for a while…but that they *always* came back, and usually sooner rather than later.

One small blessing was that at least the figures did not interfere with Becky's patient physically — if, indeed, it was possible for them to do so in the first place — but simply moved around just outside his personal space, always watching and waiting.

Think about that for a minute. Imagine what it must feel

like to be constantly in the presence of such figures, getting very little peace. There was no such thing as quiet time, as the black shapes would always be there at the fringes of your vision, not interfering with you directly, but disturbing you by virtue of their very presence.

Imagine having no respite from them, no sanctuary whatsoever – not in your bedroom, bathroom, out in the streets…not anywhere. It is distressing to think what this poor man must have felt like, dealing with their presence day in, day out. Whether they were paranormal entities of some kind or nothing more than figments of his imagination is almost irrelevant — they were real to him, and that is really all that matters in the end.

As she spoke to her patient and got him to speak about his experiences, an intriguing development came to light. Unsurprisingly, this gentleman suffered from a number of emotional disturbances and imbalances. He was sufficiently self-aware to notice that as his emotional state became increasingly unstable, the shadow figures would hang around him for longer periods of time. The more upset he was, the closer they were and the longer they stuck around. One is forced to wonder whether this was a manifestation of his mental illness, or alternatively if a certain something or other was attracted to his turbulent emotional state and was somehow able to feed off it.

There is a well-documented correlation between negative emotional energy and paranormal activity — activity of the more disturbing kind — and it may well be that something unpleasant, a form of psychic parasite if you will, could be drawn to those who are deeply upset as a moth is drawn to a flame.

Things got so oppressive that the man would no longer leave his house, and ended up confined within the same four walls day in and day out. This only worsened his downward spiral, and while Becky does not know how things ultimately turned out, one suspects that this story would not have a happy ending unless something was done to break the cycle of suffering that he was forced to endure.

I asked Becky straight up whether she believed the man was simply hallucinating, or whether he was indeed experiencing something that was paranormal in nature. After starting out with the caveat that there is no way to know something with one hundred percent certainty in the field of paranormal phenomena — a statement I would wholeheartedly agree with — she concluded that in her opinion, her patient probably *was* seeing what he claimed to see. That was her gut instinct, and while it might only be a hunch, it is one that comes on the back of many years' experience as a paranormal investigator.

"I had worked with him for several years," she explained, "and unlike some patients, where it was pretty obvious that they really just needed to be on different meds or get their doses adjusted, in this case I really do think that he was experiencing something paranormal."

The truth is, it is impossible to say for sure. Shortly after their meeting, Becky relocated to Iowa. Concerned for his wellbeing, she kept tabs on her patient as best she could. The last she heard, he was admitted to a psychiatric ward because he suffered a breakdown and was judged to be too unstable to live alone…if, indeed, he ever truly *was* alone in that house.

We can only hope that this unfortunate man finally found some measure of relief from the shadowy figures that constantly plagued and tormented him throughout his life.

CHAPTER SIXTEEN
A Call for Help

I was attending the annual *Scarefest* horror convention held in Lexington, Kentucky one year, giving a couple of paranormally-themed lectures and signing books. One afternoon, a lady approached my table and cast an eye over the range of books that I was selling. She picked up a copy of *The World's Most Haunted Hospitals* and began flipping through the pages.

"My name's Ashley and I'm a registered nurse," she explained by way of introduction. "And when it comes to haunted hospitals, I've had a few experiences of my own…"

Naturally I was intrigued, and we began chatting. The weekend was a busy one, and we agreed that I would connect with her once it was over in order to hear some of her stories.

It was a few weeks later when things finally slowed down enough for us to talk, but as soon as she began telling me her story, I realized that it had been well worth the wait.

Originally a sixth-grade history teacher, Ashley soon realized that she was not cut out for the classroom. Having always felt a strong desire to help people, she found herself drawn to nursing school, and after graduating has spent the past six years working as an RN.

She describes herself as a sensitive with "a little bit of a gift," capable of seeing spirits in certain instances. Ashley likes to think of herself as a "baby medium" (a medium in the early stages of development, not a medium that communicates with babies!) and says that she has been somewhat sensitive since the age of four. Unlike most of us, who stop talking to what our parents presume to be imaginary friends at a fairly young age, Ashley never grew out of it — something for which she is very grateful.

Paranormal field investigation has become a full-blown passion for her, to the point where she carries out a couple of investigations every month.

When I asked whether this sensitivity has affected her career in any way, she simply laughed, explaining that her office building overlooks a large cemetery. Sometimes, when she is meeting with her supervisor and colleagues, Ashley feels her gaze being drawn out toward that graveyard.

"What is it? Are you okay?" her boss will invariably ask. To which she replies that everything is fine, and that things are 'wandering around over there.' Ashley's gift doesn't seem to bother anybody in her workplace at all; it is simply taken at face value, and not made a big deal of.

The first week that Ashley started working there, she noticed a young girl in a Victorian-era dress standing beneath the branches of a large tree in the cemetery. Naturally, she went over to take a closer look. The spirit of the young girl seemed surprised that Ashley was able to see her, and while she initially got spooked (for want of a better word) and hid from the nurse, eventually she began to show a reciprocal interest of her own and started to keep a closer eye on Ashley herself.

"Spirit people know who can see them and who can't," she explains. "Don't ask me how they do it, but they can somehow tap into the gift of those who can perceive them. They know when I'm aware of their presence."

I had just had a similar discussion with a paranormal investigator, psychic medium, and registered nurse named Robbin a few days before (Robbin's stories were detailed earlier in this book). She had said much the same thing — that when she was able to see them, the spirits instinctively seemed to know that Robbin was following them around.

Reactions varied. Some entities were apparently fine with the idea, while others took the equivalent of evasive action, disappearing to parts unknown.

Many of Ashley's experiences stem from her time spent working in the Intensive Care Unit, a place which sees a high volume of truly critical patients. Despite the most skillful care of the highly-capable ICU providers, not all of the patients make it.

At the first hospital in which she worked, the ICU had a total of six separate overflow rooms for extra patients. When things got busy and those rooms filled up, the additional patients were sent to trauma department rooms; in return, when the trauma department was full, any spare ICU rooms were used as overflow for trauma patients. On such efficiencies are hospitals run across the world.

During those times when the ICU was relatively quiet, such as the lull between holidays, the extra rooms were closed off and temporarily shut down, just waiting to be needed again.

It was three weeks before Christmas. The spike in activity seen around Thanksgiving had passed, and the Christmas-time mayhem had yet to begin, so the block of rooms was being held in stasis.

An elderly gentleman was brought to the ICU in order to await an organ transplant. His need was dire, and unfortunately no suitable replacement organ could be found in time for him. The man's health deteriorated rapidly, and despite the best efforts of the ICU staff, he was soon placed on life support.

His prognosis was grim, and there was no improvement in his condition. After consultation with his next of kin, the doctors determined that the only option left to them was to remove him from life support. This is never a decision that is taken lightly, but when it is deemed necessary, it is always in the best interests of the patient.

He was transferred to one of the six rooms in the annex, where he was the only patient, and made as comfortable as possible while nature took its course. The elderly man passed away peacefully, without any suffering, and his body was taken away and put into the hands of the morticians.

A week passed. With the last remaining patient having gone from the annex, it was closed off once again. Things were still slow at the hospital, and the nurses made a point of savoring the precious down-time. They knew that Christmas was just a few days away, which meant that the ICU would be full up again in no time at all.

It was a long, slow night shift. Ashley was sitting at the nurse's station, doing her very best not to fall asleep.

Suddenly, the call light in one of the annex patient rooms lit up.

"That's strange," her fellow nurse remarked. "There are no patients back there."

"I'll go take a look," Ashley said, glad of an excuse to get up and move around. She checked all six rooms. Every single one was empty, and most were dark...except for the room where the call button had been pushed. Its main light was on.

From the minute she first set foot in the room, she was overcome with an eerie sensation, one that was hard for her to put into words. She stood there for a moment, trying to figure out what was causing it.

The longer she waited, the more strongly she became convinced that if she happened to turn around, somebody would be standing right behind her.

Finally, Ashley canceled the call button and switched out the overhead light. She went back to the nurse's station.

"What was it?" her colleague asked.

"I don't know," Ashley shrugged. "There's nobody back there."

She picked up a book and began to read. Fifteen minutes passed by. The call button pinged on again, as evidence by a light on the phone at the nurse's station. They looked at one another. This time, *both* nurses went back to check it out.

As before, the room was completely empty. They reset the call button and tried to convince one another that it was probably a fault with the equipment.

Ten minutes later, it lit up again, for the third time.

The call button worked by placing a phone call to the nurse's station phone. Despite knowing full well that the patient room was empty, Ashley's colleague reached out and picked up the phone.

"Hello…can I help you?" She paused, then put her hand over the mouthpiece. "Ashley, I can hear footsteps walking around back there in the room!"

Both women knew that this was the room in which the last patient had died. Ashley agreed to go back there once more. The main light was back on. Not a soul was to be seen. She freely admits to having gotten a little freaked out by this point, but nevertheless she looked all around to make sure that there was nobody to be found.

Except this time, there was. She turned to see a shadow figure standing in front of the window. As she took another step forward into the room, the figure instantly disappeared.

Over the next several days, there were multiple sightings

of this same shadow figure. They were always extremely brief in duration, little more than a glimpse, and it is intriguing to note that every one of them took place between 2:30 and 3:00 in the morning.

It would have been intriguing if this was the approximate time at which the elderly gentleman had passed away, but that turned out not to be the case – he had died at 1:15 in the morning. Nevertheless, one must wonder why the shadow figure was always encountered within the same thirty-minute window of time.

Unusual electrical problems are nothing new when it comes to haunted hospitals (or other types of haunted location, for that matter). Ashley recalls the time she worked in a facility in which a patient had recently died. The lights in the patient's room switched themselves off at a very fast rate, until the room gained something of a reputation for being haunted.

Maintenance technicians came regularly to troubleshoot the call switch, and went away stumped. Replacing the various electrical components failed to make any difference whatsoever – the disconcerting calls for help continued.

There is no doubt at all in Ashley's mind who was responsible. She remains convinced that the shadow figure was the spirit of the old man who died in that room, a spirit that was still earthbound for some reason and was trying to attract attention from the nurses.

Small wonder that the room always felt a little 'off' to Ashley after her experiences there. She did not possess the ability to help the shadow man move on, and found herself experiencing a tightness in her chest whenever she went into that specific room.

Shortly afterward, she moved on to a different hospital. One wonders whether the spirit of the elderly gentlemen still watches over that room, and likes to call for the nurses in the middle of the night…

Ashley's next hospital was located close to the site of a Civil War battlefield. Its location provides a compelling reason for the ghost stories associated with the hospital, particularly the multiple sightings of female apparitions all dressed in the garb of nurses from that period.

She found herself working day shifts in the ICU, and vividly remembers one patient whose multiple illnesses were far beyond curing. After a discussion with the man's family, it was agreed that the next best step was to transfer him upstairs from the ICU to palliative care, where he could be made comfortable until the end came.

The gentleman passed away later that night. The following morning, when Ashley returned to work, she ran into the priest who had administered the Last Rites to him.

"Can I please talk to those of you who took care of this gentleman?" the priest asked. "I have quite a story to share with you…"

Gathering the care team together in the nurse's lounge, he explained that the night before, the patient's entire family had gathered around his bed in order to be with him when he passed. The on-duty nurse told the family that she would step out for a while in order to give them a little privacy, instructing them to call her if they needed anything.

About an hour later, one of the family members emerged and came to the nurse's station.

"What can I do for you?" the duty nurse asked.

"This is really a little strange," said the family member, refusing to meet the nurse's eye. "We know that he is no longer breathing and his heart has stopped, but…well, he's standing in the corner of the room."

"He's…standing in the corner of the room?" the nurse repeated, not sure exactly what she was being told. She knew that grief could do strange things to people, and there really wasn't much in the medical field that had the power to surprise her any more.

She was about to be proven wrong.

"That's right. Perhaps it would be best if you just came and saw for yourself…"

When the nurse entered the room, she saw the old man's body laying motionless in the bed, surrounded by his nearest and dearest. The cardiac monitor screen showed three flat lines, indicating that all electrical activity in his heart had stopped.

And there the patient was, just as the family member had insisted, standing in the corner of the room.

The nurse looked at him. He looked back.

Nobody spoke.

In all fairness, this wasn't something that was ever discussed in nursing school! How can you possibly prepare somebody for an encounter with the spirit of a dead patient? All eight members of the deceased's family *plus* the duty nurse maintained that they were able to see his apparition.

Finally regaining her composure, the nurse went to call the hospital priest, who arrived a few minutes later. After leading the family in offering up both a prayer and a blessing over their loved one's body, the man's ghost was seen to walk across the room and disappear through the closed door.

This is one of the more remarkable accounts of an apparition sighting that I have ever come across in my career. The number of witnesses – eight family members, a nurse and a priest – is impressive. The story was told directly to Ashley by that selfsame priest.

Yet as a paranormal investigator, I would be remiss if I did not ask the following question: with the apparition being visible for a prolonged period of time, what was to prevent just *one* of them from taking out their phone and attempting to take a photograph or some capture some video footage of the spirit?

Flipping it around, the priest and the nurse would have no motivation to make up such a story. The events surrounding the dying man and his subsequent apparition were never made public, and if anything, the hospital authorities would have worked to suppress them, rather than use them in order to try and generate publicity. What reason would there have been for the priest and the nurse to lie or exaggerate?

I can think of none, and so, as is so often the case when it comes to the paranormal, we are maddeningly left with more questions than answers.

CHAPTER SEVENTEEN
A Prankster in the Morgue

A hospital's operating theater is the place in which surgeries great and small are carried out, ranging from the most minor of elective procedures all the way up to major life-saving surgical interventions. Even those supposedly routine surgeries carry a degree of risk, however, particularly if a patient is either on the older side or has an underlying comorbidity, such as diabetes or heart disease. These are factors that every surgeon must take into account before deciding whether or not to operate.

In this particular case, the surgical team was going to remove a blood clot from the body of a lady in her mid-sixties. The clot was blocking one of her arteries, and needed to be taken out.

Although one might expect the lady to be nervous, she was actually very upbeat, happily chatting away and joking with the surgical team as they prepped her. The same could not be said of Amanda, one of the nurses who was assisting in theater on this particular day. For some reason, she had a sense of foreboding concerning this patient. It was just an instinct, but as irrational as that might have seemed, it caused her to look the surgeon directly in the eye.

"Take extra good care of her, won't you?"

The surgeon shot her a look which implied that she might have gone stark, raving mad. As the anesthesiologist attached a syringe to the patient's IV line and began to administer the sedative and anesthetic drugs that would put the patient under and keep her there for a while, Amanda gave her hand a warm squeeze.

"Don't worry," she said, projecting a sense of good cheer that she did not truly feel. "I'll make you a nice hot cup of tea when the surgery's done."

The room was filled with the reassuring sound of the cardiac monitor bleeping in time to the patient's heartbeat, and the steady, mechanical hiss of the ventilator pushing air into her lungs through an endotracheal tube. The lady was well and truly out now, the drugs having done their job well, and her vital signs looked good and stable…

…for about ten minutes.

A strident alarm began to screech. All eyes turned to the cardiac monitor, where the patient's heart rhythm had changed from a continuous sequence of healthy heartbeats into a harsh, chaotic mess.

All highly-trained professionals, the surgical team

sprang into action. The cardiac dysrhythmia was defibrillated, but without any success. Adrenaline and antidysrhythmic drugs were pushed into the patient's veins. Most important of all, CPR was started in an attempt to keep her life blood circulating.

None of it did any good.

Amanda had begun to suspect that things were not going to end well when she looked up for a second and saw three spirit people standing unobtrusively in the shadows along the back wall of the operating theater. They had followed the patient in, but she had been too busy attending to her duties to pay them much attention. Now she began to suspect that they were either members of the deceased's family, or possibly her spirit guides; either way, it appeared that they had come to help her transition across to the other side.

The medical team did their very best to resuscitate their patient, but unfortunately their efforts were in vain. She died on the operating table, much to the consternation of everybody concerned — particularly the surgeon, who shot Amanda a look that seemed to say: *Why did you ask me to take extra good care of her — what could you possibly have known that I didn't?*

Untying and removing his surgical mask, he said, "You

can go and break the news to the family. They're in the waiting room."

Amanda stood her ground. "No, I will *not*. You're the doctor, I'm the nurse. It's not my place to go out there and inform them that they have lost their loved one during a routine operation."

Not used to being pushed back on, the surgeon stormed out of the operating room and went to deliver the bad news to an understandably distraught family.

The surgical team were dejected, but like the true professionals they were, they all knew that the show must go on. There were other surgeries scheduled immediately after this one, and so they worked to clean up the operating theater and get it ready for the next patient. Amanda and the assistant Nursing Unit Manager (NUM) were assigned to take the body of the deceased lady down to the morgue, which was located in the basement of the hospital.

Hospital rules stated that dead bodies were not permitted to be wheeled through hospital corridors and elevators with a sheet covering them, despite what Hollywood movies may have us believe, and so they had no choice but to place her on a gurney with an oxygen mask over her face and a hair covering on top of her head. Normally, the orderlies would have made special arrangements, but none were available at that time. It was bad form for them to do what they were doing, but the surgeons were insistent that they needed to get the next surgery rolling, and so the two nurses had no choice.

Now that the bad news had gotten out, other members of the deceased lady's family were coming to the hospital in order to be together. Amanda and her partner had a couple of near-misses, coming perilously close to running into some of them as they negotiated the hospital hallways with the dead body in tow. Only some quickly thought-out backtracking prevented them from making a bad situation even worse.

Complicating matters even further was the fact that the spirit of the deceased patient, showing a decidedly macabre sense of humor, was following along behind them. Amanda could sense her back there, occasionally tapping her on the shoulder, laughing in her ear, and chuckling, "Hurry it up, dear — you did promise me a cup of tea, you know!"

"Stop it," Amanda mumbled under her breath, not wanting her colleague to hear her apparently talking to herself. She noticed anyway.

"Are you okay?" the NUM asked.

No, Amanda was *not* OK. She was resisting the urge to snap, *"Cut me some slack, I'm getting hassled by a dead woman, so chill the hell out!"* Instead, she just nodded. She was starting to feel the pressure, and the dead lady had chosen the worst possible time to start joking around.

They finally made it to the morgue without any further complications. After turning over their patient's body to the attendant there, Amanda and the NUM headed back the way they had come.

Amanda couldn't resist taking a quick look back over her shoulder. The lady's spirit was standing in the morgue doorway, clutching at her sides and laughing at her own joke. She threw Amanda a wink, waved good-bye, and was suddenly surrounded in a halo of bright light. Other figures were visible inside that light, but beyond that, Amanda could not see.

The spirit entity turned and walked into the light, which then winked out as if somebody had switched a flashlight beam off, heading on to whatever awaits us once this physical life is over.

CHAPTER EIGHTEEN
The Bravest Yeti

Like most paranormal investigators, I have taken on a diverse range of cases over the course of my career. Some have been uneventful and relatively mundane in nature. Others turned out to be the real deal, genuine hauntings that continue to defy conventional explanation.

Throughout all of this, I have encountered a number of truly memorable, remarkable people. There was the single mother who lived in a historic former prison, which was once used to incarcerate those accused of witchcraft. She claimed to have endured years of hellish treatment at the hands of the restless spirits which haunted the place.

Then there was the owner of a haunted Italian restaurant, who felt an uncanny affinity for the spirit of a former owner of the building, along with the ghostly little girl who liked to run playfully through the customer area, playing hide-and-go-seek underneath the dining tables.

There was also the spirit of a serial killer, the man known as the I-70 Strangler, who murdered somewhere between seventeen and thirty men — possibly more — during his reign of terror across the state of Indiana during the 1990s. I swam in the pool located in the basement of his house while investigating claims of a haunting there, and was rewarded with a blood-chilling growl for my trouble.

Yet one particular encounter stands out from all the rest. It is the one that I will never, ever forget, not even if I live to be a hundred, and the story is so remarkable that it was the inspiration behind the writing of this book. It involves ghosts and a haunting, yes, but to focus on just the paranormal aspects of it would be missing the point.

I am no stranger to ghostly encounters; in fact, one might say that they have become my bread and butter over the years, the reason that I spend so much of my free time prowling the hallways of haunted locations, attempting to capture evidence of paranormal activity and to document the lives of those who came before us. But what has stayed with me where this particular haunting is concerned, has less to do with the spirits, and everything to do with the sheer courage of the young man who encountered them.

His name is Kyle.

He is my hero. And I suspect that after hearing his story, he will be your hero too.

I have been fortunate enough to meet a lot of heroes in my life.

Few of them are of the flashy, razzle-dazzle, Hollywood action hero variety. Some are the firefighters I lived and worked alongside, who thought nothing of crawling into a burning building in order to search for victims inside. Others are the EMTs and paramedics I continue to serve with, men and women who are paid an absolute pittance — often less than they would be able to make flipping burgers at a fast food joint — and work long hours, while all the time getting verbally and physically abused. Not to mention the fact that they see things which no human being should ever have to see, things that cannot be unseen no matter how much they might want to.

Then there are the teachers, who strive to bring the light of knowledge into an ever-darkening world; the doctors and nurses who fight against all odds in order to save a life and aid in their patient's recovery and recuperation; and then there are those who dedicate themselves to caring for a sick or elderly relative, or look after a child with special needs.

The list goes on and on.

The one thing that all of these people have in common with one another is courage. Not the 'on your feet and charge an enemy machine gun nest' sort of courage demonstrated by soldiers, but rather the quiet, unassuming variety that tackles each difficult day as it comes, day in and day out, sometimes for years.

This is a special kind of bravery, and while it may not be glamorous, it is no less heroic for that. One man who possesses this type of courage in abundance is somebody who I am fortunate to call my friend. That is Kyle, and I have been given the great privilege of helping to share his story with you.

I first learned of Kyle through a professional association. Back in 2009, I graduated from one of Colorado's better-known paramedic academies. Nowadays, almost ten years later, I go back to my alma mater six times a year in order to teach the new crop of students. It's an honor to be asked to help shape the next generation of paramedics, and I can still recall exactly what it felt like to be sitting in their seats, staring up at the instructor and taking reams of notes on whatever was the medical subject of the day.

One of the academy course coordinators happened to have a friend who had once served as a paramedic. His son had spent the past thirteen years fighting courageously against a terminal illness — he was diagnosed with a cancerous tumor of an unknown type in 2005, when he was just ten years old.

After a great deal of testing and puzzlement on the part of some of America's top doctors, Kyle was eventually diagnosed with an extremely rare condition known as Mesenchymal Chondrosarcoma. It makes up less than one percent of all cancers worldwide. According to his physicians, the longest known life span of a patient with Mesenchymal Chondrosarcoma has been eight years...until now.

Thirteen years after his onset of symptoms, Kyle is still hanging tough.

Thirteen. Years.

As his condition progressed, and with no possibility of a cure in sight, Kyle had begun to be visited by the spirits of those children who he had befriended during his many hospital stays, all of whom had now passed away. Kyle was the only one still left alive, and with his own passing now growing closer, he believed that these visitations were a sign that his friends were looking over him, helping to ease the burden of the difficult journey that he was undertaking.

Kyle's father contacted me by email and asked whether I would be interested in paying Kyle a visit. He would like to tell his story and discuss it with somebody who had a background in the paranormal.

To be totally honest, I was a little nervous about the idea. What if I said the wrong thing? I didn't want to take the risk of upsetting Kyle or his family if my somewhat skeptical approach challenged their beliefs. But at the same time, I knew deep down that making an excuse not to go would have been nothing other than cowardice on my part. By all accounts, Kyle was a very intelligent young man, and the more I thought about it, the more I realized that after all that he had been through, the skepticism of a paranormal investigator was unlikely to even register as a blip on his radar of things to be concerned about.

Looking back now with the benefit of hindsight, I am so glad that I did not make that excuse. If I had, I would have deprived myself of the experience of meeting one of the most remarkable human beings I have ever known in my entire life.

I made the two-hour drive from my workplace to Kyle's home, just south of Denver, one night after finishing up my duties for the day. My mind was racing, churning over and over and wondering just what exactly I was going to say to him. There is a certain inherent awkwardness when it comes to speaking with those who are terminally ill. I had experienced it before, not just with my medical patients, but also when I was sitting alongside my own dear mum during her last days. She had been diagnosed with terminal cancer, originating in her lungs but then metastasizing up to her brain, as that insidious disease is prone to doing.

Night by night I would sit beside her bed, holding her hand and talking to her during the few lucid intervals she had between drifting off to sleep and incoherently rambling because of the strange effects that the cancer exerted upon her brain. Sometimes she was as sharp as a tack, and we chatted nostalgically about happier times gone by, and some of the things that were going on in the world outside the confines of her bedroom. I told her how much I loved her (though never often enough) but when it came down to small talk, it all seemed so, well, *small*. When your weeks and then finally your days are truly numbered, why would you want to talk about mundane, everyday matters?

But I finally figured out that the minutiae of everyday life had been *exactly* what she wanted to talk about. My mother didn't spend what little remaining time she had left in going over the more momentous events of her life, such as getting married, divorced, or raising a child — at least, if she did, she never mentioned it to me, or to any of the palliative care staff that attended to her needs. Instead, she wanted to talk about what was going on in her favorite soap operas, and which family members and work colleagues had visited her that day. There was no discussion of life, the afterlife (something which she wholeheartedly believed in) or the grand meaning of it all. Instead, we laughed and cried together about the most minor things imaginable.

I wondered whether Kyle would be the same way. Part of me rather hoped that he would be. When it came down to the great philosophical questions, I felt woefully unqualified to answer them. Having spent more than half my life conducting paranormal investigations at supposedly haunted locations on both sides of the Atlantic, I definitely had some opinions on the subject of ghosts and what happens to us after we die, but that's all that they were — opinions. It wasn't as if I was an expert, because there is no such thing as an expert in this particular field. There is only experience and conjecture.

Kyle and his family lived in a nice home in an ordinary residential neighborhood. His dad met me at the door, shaking my hand and leading me upstairs to the bedroom where Kyle spent almost all of his time. It looked just like any other young man's bedroom I had ever seen. Kyle himself was sitting up in bed, and offered me a cheerful greeting when his dad introduced us.

Propped up on some pillows, he had a pretty sweet computer rig mounted on a bespoke desk that straddled his bed. Kyle, a handsome young chap whose nickname was 'Yeti' (don't ask) was also an avid video gamer, something we both had in common. That played directly into the story he wanted to tell me.

He had stayed up late one night playing one of his favorite online games. Finally tired, Kyle shut down his computer and settled back to try and get some sleep. Before he could close his eyes, he was amazed when two human-like figures came into his room from the hallway outside. Each was somewhere between seven and eight feet tall, and emanated a golden-whitish glow.

As he got over his initial shock, Kyle sat up on his pillows and began to scrutinize the two entities. He realized that they hadn't actually *walked* in the same way that human beings do; instead, they had seemed to glide, coming gracefully through the doorway without ever moving their legs. The motion was extremely smooth, looking ever so slightly unnatural, and absolutely silent. No footsteps accompanied the two figures.

Kyle had been suffering a great deal of pain in his left

cheek for quite some time, the result of the surgical removal of a tumor. The closest of the two figures approached his bed and extended an arm, resting its hand gently upon his cheek. A sensation of great warmth flooded through the side of Kyle's face. Best of all, the pain immediately went away.

"I had no feeling at all of being scared," Kyle recalled later. "No feeling of anything bad. It was all very peaceful and relaxing."

There were no recognizable facial features on either of the two beings, so it was impossible for him to tell whether they were male, female, or something else. Yet when the closer of the two laid its hand upon him, Kyle distinctly heard a woman's voice say the words: "The third time will be the final time."

That made me lean forward in my chair, intrigued. "What do you think that she meant?" I asked.

Kyle had bravely fought a life-and-death struggle with his aggressive illness in 2006 and 2010. Now it was back for round three, having returned in 2016, and after thinking about it, Kyle had come to believe that the female entity was letting him know that this was going to be his last battle with it.

Considering that our meeting took place in the summer

of 2018, I realized that meant Kyle had been fighting cancer for over two years without a break. I stood in absolute awe of this young man's courage, the sheer guts it took to do what he had done.

"The first time I got cancer, they [the surgeons] took it out. The second time, they took it out again. But this time, they can't," he told me, very matter-of-factly. "It spread too quickly. This time I'm terminal."

"The cancer metastasized to his lungs," Kyle's dad explained.

It has long been accepted that animals, particularly household pets such as cats and dogs, seem to have some sort of sensitivity where ghosts are concerned. Most pet owners have experienced the disconcerting sight of their animal staring intently toward an empty corner of the room, or some spot on the staircase, and suddenly gotten a bad case of the chills. This makes it all the more surprising that Kyle's dog, curled up contentedly alongside him, didn't react in the slightest to the unexpected arrival of the two visitors. When I first entered Kyle's room, on the other hand, I got the full once-over from the pooch before being allowed to sit down with his human.

Not wanting to trample on his beliefs, I nevertheless felt

the need to ask Kyle whether this could all have been just a dream. "I was absolutely wide awake," he insisted, before adding that he wore an Apple iWatch, and one of its features was to track his sleep periods. When he checked it after the encounter, the watch showed that he was still awake.

There was also the undeniable fact that the debilitating pain in Kyle's cheek, something that he had been suffering from for quite some time, disappeared immediately after the entity's touch had suffused some kind of warmth through it.

Dreams do not cure pain…of the physical kind, at least.

As he told me of this remarkable encounter, there was a surety and a certainty in Kyle's manner that was just so impressive. He was facing the end of his life — "This time I'm terminal," he had said — without complaint or any sign of fear. I doubted that I possessed that level of courage. I suspect that most of us do not.

I shared with him and his dad the fact that cancer aggressively metastasizing throughout the body was what had killed my mother. They both listened patiently as I told them about the visits she had gotten in the night from long-dead family members. The hospice nursing staff had told me all about it. Such apparent visitations are not at all uncommon, and I have heard numerous accounts from those kind and compassionate souls who work in the arena of palliative care. While some skeptics may dismiss such experiences as the hallucinations of a dying brain, I hold the belief that they are just as likely to be exactly what they appear to be: our deceased loved ones returning from the next world in order to help ease the transition from this one. No matter which explanation turns out to be true, it cannot be denied that such encounters are almost always found to be deeply comforting for those who experience them.

"There are some nurses that see a kind of 'grim reaper' or 'angel of death,'" Kyle told me. He had obviously been doing his research. "It comes in a different form for different witnesses. Sometimes it's a little boy. Sometimes it's an old man or woman. When people see it, it usually means a patient is going to die."

I had heard those stories too, and had learned that such apparitions were well-documented in the paranormal case lore. In fact, one of my favorite haunted locations — the old Tooele Valley Hospital in Tooele, Utah — was said to have such a ghost, in the form of a dark man that was seen going into the rooms of those who would die the next day…that is, if the nursing staff who related the story to the host of the TV show *Ghost Adventures* are to be believed.

While some might find the idea of a harbinger of death frightening, I can easily see how others might actually take some degree of comfort from it.

"You seem totally fearless to me, Kyle," I said, still in awe of just how well he was handling his situation. "Does the thought of dying worry you at all?"

He shook his head emphatically. "I'm not afraid. I'll go when it's my time," he told me without the slightest hesitation.

"Kyle knows he's going to a special place," his dad chimed in. "Away from the cancer. It took Johns Hopkins, Sloan-Kettering (a highly-regarded cancer center) and the CDC a good *ten years* to try and figure out what his illness was, and they *still* don't know enough about it."

Kyle's father went on to give a list of the other maladies that had come in the wake of the cancer, including a failed gallbladder and necrosis to Kyle's skull, in which the bones of his face were eaten away and had to be surgically treated. Yet despite being the medical equivalent of a punching bag, Kyle had fought back heroically, going out and raising thousands of dollars for the St Baldrick's Foundation by shaving his head for charity — during those seven years when he actually *had* any hair left, thanks to the cancer treatments.

To my mind, this young man is the very definition of a hero. I have never felt more awed in the presence of another person in my entire life.

"Were the two glowing figures the only strange thing you've encountered here at home?" I asked, bringing the conversation back around to the paranormal before I found myself bursting into tears.

It turned out that they were not. Ever since they had visited him, Kyle had begun to see a dark shadow figure walking past his doorway, in the hallway outside his bedroom. The figure never comes into his room, never interacts with Kyle, and doesn't show any sign of awareness that he is even there. He isn't sure of its identity, and I found it to be intriguing. Had the encounter with the glowing figures opened some kind of doorway or portal that allowed other spirit entities to come through? There seemed to be a sudden influx of paranormal activity in the household since they had arrived and the female visitor had told Kyle that the third time would be the final time.

Not one to sit back passively and let life simply happen to him, Kyle decided that he would much rather attempt to search for some answers of his own — in other words, he wanted to conduct his own private, one-man paranormal investigation. Although he had no doubts whatsoever about the reality of the haunting, he would have liked nothing more than to capture some evidence that might validate the truth of his experiences in the eyes of others.

To that end, Kyle began taking photographs in his bedroom whenever he felt as though something strange might be afoot. As we sat side by side, he showed some of those pictures to me, swiping through them on his tablet. One which he found intriguing seemed to show a human-like face (complete with a tongue sticking out) floating in the air at the end of his bed.

"This is the tech aspect that I don't really understand," his father laughed.

Kyle asked me what I thought of the photos. I was silent for a minute. After giving them due consideration, I concluded that they were most likely pareidolia, plain and simple. But some people become extremely emotionally invested in what they believe to be photographs of ghosts. In my side job as a tour guide at a very haunted hotel up in the Rocky Mountains, my fellow tour guides and I see this all the time. Some guests will pitch an absolute fit if my colleagues and I tell them that the so-called 'spirit orb' they captured in our rather dusty tunnel system is, in fact, exactly that — dust, reflecting the camera's flash backward into the lens and causing that characteristic orb effect that every experienced paranormal investigator knows on sight.

I weighed up the pros and cons for a moment, but soon decided that there was only one right answer. Kyle and his dad were asking me for my professional opinion, and I owed them the truth, no matter how unpalatable they might find it.

"I think that it's basically just a natural light effect," I said, choosing my words with great care. "Our brains are wired to want to interpret random patterns as having some kind of meaning, turning a jumble of light and shadow into what they think are faces or human bodies."

To my great relief, both Kyle and his dad were completely unfazed by my explanation. If they were even the slightest bit disappointed, they certainly never showed any sign of it. That spoke volumes to me about their willingness to consider possible alternative explanations to the paranormal solution. They had not lost sight of the need to keep an open mind, no matter how fantastic Kyle's experiences seemed to be. My level of respect for them both climbed even higher on the strength of that.

"This is a brand-new house," Kyle's dad pointed out.

"There's no reason for it to be haunted. At least, not that we're aware of."

"Unless it's built on an old Native American burial ground, like half of Colorado seems to be," I chuckled. "But to be serious for a minute, I agree with you. If this house is haunted, then the reason behind it is most likely going to be what happened to Kyle."

"Well, he *is* the last survivor." Turning to his son, Kyle's dad asked whether he had tried taking any photos when his ghostly friends turned up. Kyle replied that he hadn't, which made sense to me. These were the boys and girls he had undergone cancer treatment with, had laughed and played with, and often suffered alongside, before finally losing them all one by one until he was the only one left. When they returned to visit him in his bedroom late at night, it must have been a deeply emotional experience for him. The last thing on his mind would have been reaching for his cell phone in order to start snapping pictures of them.

Our discussion turned once more toward those apparent visitations. Kyle related an experience that had happened to him when he had been admitted to the Intensive Care Unit at the hospital after his second round of cancer treatment.

Kyle's mom spent every hour that she could spare

visiting him there in the ICU. One day, as she was standing at his bedside, Kyle caught sight of an old woman standing quietly behind her, hardly moving against the background of sterile walls and medical monitoring equipment. He did not recognize the woman. Kyle was hooked up to so many tubes and wires that he had the strength to do little more than just lie there.

After being discharged from the ICU, he mentioned the appearance of the stranger to his mother, asking who the old lady had been. She had absolutely no idea what he was talking about. So far as she was concerned, that had been nobody else in the ICU when she was visiting.

Not long afterward, Kyle was idly leafing through some old family photographs. Suddenly, there she was. In one of them, the same old lady could be seen, smiling happily away for the camera.

She was Kyle's grandmother on his mother's side, somebody that he had never met during her lifetime. In other words, his mom's mom was standing right behind her, something of which Kyle's mother was completely unaware.

Such experiences are hardly unusual. Kyle brought up the conversations my own mother had had with deceased family members as she lay dying in a hospice bed, saying that the two experiences sounded quite similar. I had to agree.

Having spoken to numerous psychic mediums over the years, I have often heard it said that during times of crisis, particularly those in which a life hangs in the balance, the spirits of our deceased loved ones draw nearer to us, lending us their strength and emotional support. How difficult must it be for a mother to watch over her son under such harrowing circumstances? Small wonder, then, that her own mother should have dropped by in order to support her daughter during a time of great turmoil.

Kyle has lost his sense of smell and his sense of taste. He does remember what it was like to eat his favorite food, is able to recall those things from his memory…but as Kyle told me about that, in a very matter-of-fact way, I found myself thinking about just how much I took for granted in my own life. When I went home later that night, dinner would be waiting for me in the microwave. No matter what it was that my wife had prepared, I would be able to savor the aroma and the taste of it. Kyle would never have that luxury ever again. He was totally incapable of appreciating food in the same way that you and I can.

Right there and then, I resolved never to complain about a meal ever again.

"I'm starting to forget what those tastes were like though," he said, a little wistfully. "But there are some benefits. I can eat spicy hot wings without them burning my mouth out."

Having lost something so fundamental, Kyle was still able to look on the bright side of things. It was so bloody moving.

"I'm here with family right now, able to spend time with the people I love," Kyle said. "That's what really matters. I don't think about too much else."

Boy, did this guy have his priorities straight! Most of us sleepwalk through life, going about our trivial business from day to day, never really appreciating the little things that we are gifted with — the things that, in the end, turn out to be the most important things of all.

Family. Friends. Love.

Perhaps because he had gone through a living hell, my new friend was wise beyond his years. It struck me that we could all benefit from taking a leaf out of his book when it came to living our lives and figuring out what was truly important.

"There's lightning out there," Kyle said, breaking my chain of thought. Puzzled, I looked outside through the window. I hadn't seen any flashes.

"Kyle can *feel* lightning, before it actually strikes," his dad explained. Just like the progressive sensory loss that he was experiencing, this newfound ability had come about because of his illness and ongoing treatment. Sure enough, just a few minutes later, there came the boom of thunder and a flash of lightning. Kyle's prediction had been right on the money.

It was dark by the time I said my goodbyes and left, with a promise that I would come back again and hang out with Kyle in the future. The two-hour drive home passed by in what seemed like no time at all; I had so much to think about after our time together.

I didn't play music or listen to an audiobook, as I usually did on longer drives. There was no way that my mind could concentrate on either of them. I was totally preoccupied with my meeting with Kyle and his father. It had, for want of a better term, hit me right in the feels.

It had been a long day at work before I had hit the road for Castle Rock. I'd found at least five or six things or people to complain about, be irritated by, or be resentful for. And now, here was this young man, who would have given practically *anything* in order to be able to go to a job.

I'm not ashamed to admit that before I knew it, I was crying like a baby. He was an incredible young man, a shining example of bravery and positivity, and it was all so bloody *unfair*.

If I had been put in Kyle's place, I was pretty sure that I would have been royally pissed off at the world in general and everything in it. Yet Kyle behaved with such incredible grace and dignity. He was setting an exceptional example for the rest of us. After thinking about it for the next few days, I finally came to the conclusion that there was a great deal that Kyle could teach me — a great deal that he could teach most people, in fact. He was quite the role model, exemplifying quiet courage and dignity in the face of a level of adversity that would emotionally crush most of us.

I resolved to try and follow Kyle's exmple and look at my own difficulties and challenges — which were laughably small when measured against his — in perspective.

It remains one of the most precious gifts that anybody

has ever given me.

A few months went by. The weeks spanning Halloween are always the busiest in any paranormal investigator's calendar, and although Kyle and I stayed connected on Facebook, chatting back and forth every so often, it wasn't until Thanksgiving had passed that I was able to visit him in person once more.

Kyle's illness had progressed, spreading farther and more aggressively into his lungs. The chemotherapy and other medical treatments just weren't doing much of anything to halt its spread anymore.

The day before I visited, Kyle made the difficult decision to stop undergoing those ineffective treatments, choosing instead to focus on keeping his pain in check as best as possible and remaining somewhat comfortable. It was a tough choice, one that required immense bravery to make, but ultimately the right one, I believe.

Kyle's incredible parents and his terrific big sister were one hundred percent supportive of his decision, and as I spent a little time chatting to them all in their living room, I came to respect them every bit as much as I did Kyle. They really were all in this together, closing ranks and looking out for one another. It was a wonderful thing to see.

Kyle's dad let me know in advance that Kyle had lost some of his hearing in both ears and also found it a little more difficult to talk, both side-effects of the cancer that was encroaching on different parts of his skull. We'd still be able to talk, but I needed to talk slower and louder to make myself heard. For his part, Kyle had to overcome the enormous drag factor of my English accent, so he had my complete sympathy there.

I'd written a blog post about Kyle and his paranormal experience shortly after our first meeting. This had resulted in an outpouring of cards and gifts from my friends and readers, who had also sent comic books, video games, movies, collectables, and letters expressing their best wishes. My wife, Laura, wrapped them all up in two giant gift boxes and I carried them up to his room with me. It was as though Christmas had come early — at least, a fat man had tiptoed quietly into his room and brought presents, so it was close enough for government work.

I found Kyle sitting up in bed, getting the better of yet another video game. His characteristic good mood was in full force, and it wasn't long before he was enjoying opening the gifts from well-wishers and talking about the burning issue of the day: whether the new *Aquaman* movie was going to be any good when it hit theaters.

I took a chair next to his bed and once again enjoyed laughing and joking with my friend. After a while, the conversation turned toward his paranormal experiences. He told me that one of his newer chemotherapy friends had died since our last meeting, and the young man had now begun to appear among the group of nocturnal visitors.

"How often are they coming?" I asked.

"Sometimes it's every night," Kyle said, "but it's at least every other night. When there are bad days, they come more often. Then I see them in the day time as well." By *bad days,* he meant those days on which the pain was particularly bad, or ones on which his spirits were at a very low ebb. It was the first time I'd ever heard him even hint at the fact that his terminal illness wasn't exactly a rose garden.

"Do they ever talk to you, Kyle?" I asked him.

He shook his head. "Not in words. I just know that they're watching over me, giving me comfort. I can feel it."

I had no problem believing that. Several psychic mediums I'd spoken to had told me that very thing, that the spirits of those who are near and dear to us come back at the end of our physical lives to help ease our transition across into the next life. What an immensely comforting thought that was.

The spirits of those departed kids never came into his room, he said, but rather stood outside in the hall, as though standing guard. One (not both) of the tall, glowing figures had also returned, Kyle told me. It had been on a day when he felt particularly unwell, and he had seen a number of dark shadow figures running back and forth at the top of the staircase. These weren't the spirits of his friends, but rather something else…something that he couldn't identify.

Whoever or whatever these newcomers were, they didn't feel good to Kyle. His spirit friends kept them out of his bedroom, and the only entity that entered was the luminous figure that had visited him before and said that the third time would be the last time. Once again, she was able to reduce Kyle's pain and make him feel a little bit better.

On those nights when he felt afraid or lonely, the protective, friendly spirits always managed to make him feel a little less upset. They continue to stand watch over their friend night after night, making sure that this remarkable young man is never truly alone.

When I left Kyle's home that night, I felt differently than

I had after our first visit. There were no tears this time. Instead, I was overwhelmingly struck by Kyle's positivity. He was well aware that his life was coming to an end, having gone so far as to discuss funeral arrangements with his family, and was facing it head-on like a warrior. *That* was the lesson Kyle had taught me on our second visit, without ever realizing that he had done so — the lesson that we are never truly alone, no matter how lonely or hurt we may feel.

There are always those who care for us, keeping a watchful, protective eye out for our welfare. It was just that Kyle, perhaps due to his illness and being close to the end of his life, was now actually able to see them with his own eyes.

When I stood up from his bedside, Kyle fired a parting shot that left me with some real food for thought. "Some people are going to say that the drugs are making me see things," he said, something which I knew to be absolutely true. It was a valid point for a skeptic to make. "But I've stopped taking almost all of my medications. I'm still seeing my friends coming back to visit me. So how can it be those drugs?"

He was absolutely right, I realized. Once those medications were out of his system, it would no longer be possible to use them as an explanation for his paranormal experiences. For Kyle (and also for me) it was one step closer to validating the reality of his nocturnal encounters.

As I write these words, the Christmas holidays are fast approaching. Gifts for Kyle are still coming in from well-wishers, and I am very much looking forward to visiting him for a third time early in the new year to drop them off and spend more time with him.

The responses that Kyle's story has gotten from those who have heard it continue to blow me away. When I told Kyle just how many people had written notes of support and encouragement to me on his behalf, either by means of social media or by physically mailing them, he was very much taken aback. After talking to him about it in greater detail, I realized that Kyle has literally *no ego whatsoever*. He finds it almost impossible to conceive of himself as being brave, courageous, or heroic.

"My job these days is just passing the time and being me," he said with characteristic modesty. "Nobody needs to make a big deal out of me. I'm not looking for attention. I just wanted to share my story."

But this kid (sorry, but I still think of him as a kid, which probably does him a great disservice) is nothing less than a true hero. He's raised thousands of dollars for cancer research. During his time in the hospital, he would regularly wander into the other kids' rooms and do his very best to cheer them up when they were down. Kyle is constantly thinking of others instead of himself, even though he is fully aware that his own days on this Earth are numbered.

How better do you define a hero?

There are many dark and frightening stories in this book, accounts of encounters with entities that may chill the blood. I have chosen to end the book with Kyle's story because it is, in my opinion, the most inspirational. Yes, the visits he receives from the spirits of his friends fascinate me as a paranormal investigator; yet the true point of this story is the way in which one young man serves as a role model for all of us, demonstrating the fact that while each and every one of us must die someday, it is possible for us to face that end with dignity, courage, and not give in to our fears.

Kyle, you are one of the kindest, gentlest, and bravest souls it has ever been my privilege to call my friend. Thank you for all that you have taught me, for allowing me to be a small part of your life, and to share your story with a wider audience.

You, my friend, are the very best of us.

Way to go, Yeti.

Acknowledgments

Firstly, to you, the reader: Thank you for spending your hard-earned money and valuable time in order to read this book. It is my sincere hope that you have enjoyed it, and would ask you to please consider rating the book on Amazon's website. In the current writing market, books tend to live and die by their reviews and ratings, particularly on Amazon. Your help would therefore be greatly appreciated.

Some other thanks are due to the people without whom this book would not have been possible, beginning with those who allowed me to share their stories.

Robbin Daidone
Anney Horn
Susan Fretwell
Amanda Wright-Tabone
Bill Tabone
Rick Krab
Trish Quinn
Luis Taz Cruz
Becky Carter
Ashley Wiseman

Chris Balassone, for writing the introduction

Laura, for all of her support.

A fair chunk of this book was written in the wee small hours of the morning at Coombe Abbey in England. Much love goes out to the **Sage Tribe,** with a special shout-out to **MJ** and **Duncan Dickson,** who are to blame for *everything.* Heartfelt thanks are also due to **Carl Hutchinson, Elizabeth Koert, Susan Cummins, Chris Fleming, Barri Ghai, Aaron Sagers, Karen Dahlman, Barrie John, Cal Cooper, Katrina Weidman, Dee Dee, Penny Griffiths-Morgan,** and all the other very fine people that made Sage Paracon 3 such a memorable event. I wish I could list each and every one of your names here!

My partners-in-crime **Linda** and **Jason Fellon, Anna Choate, Catlyn Keenan, Stephen Weidner, Erik Bensen, Richard Ricketts, Jill Woodward Saunderson, Susan Hatcliff, Connie Mianecki, Lesley Bridge, Gaynor Clarke, CJ Symonds, Karin Beasant,** and **Kirsten Honey** for going on so many phenomenal adventures with me this year. Here's to many more in future!

My **Asylum 49** family, still running the greatest haunt on the planet. Love you all.

Wes and the guys from **COPS**. It was great doing jail time with you, lads. Let's do it again sometime, eh?

Sarah Stream, Josh Heard, Luis Taz Cruz (again), Chris Case, Dave Schrader, and **Johnny Houser** for great times at Malvern Manor, Wizard World Iowa, and Villisca.

My brothers and sisters at **AMR Boulder, Golden,** and **Longmont,** not to mention **Boulder Rural Fire.**

Everybody at **East Drive,** Pontefract.

My para-friends and family across Britain, the U.S. and Canada. I wish there were room to thank you all personally here for all that you do.

If you feel so inclined, please visit me over at my web page, www.richardestep.net. I love to hear from readers, so drop by and say hi!

And last but by no means least, the most important people on the list: **Kyle, Marty, Ingrid,** and **Megan.** You guys are a true inspiration. Thank you for welcoming me into your home.

Much love,
Richard

Printed in Great Britain
by Amazon